BE...

Also by Ashley Black

The Cellulite Myth: It's Not Fat, It's Fascia
The Cellulite Myth Daily Companion Guide:
Your 12-Week Journey to Transformation

BE...

FROM PASSION *and* PURPOSE *to* PRODUCT *and* PROSPERITY

BE... it, then become it.
xo - Korie

FROM #1 NATIONAL BESTSELLING AUTHOR
ASHLEY BLACK *with* KORIE MINKUS
and LISA VRANCKEN

A POST HILL PRESS BOOK
ISBN: 978-1-64293-788-6
ISBN (eBook): 978-1-64293-789-3

Be...:
From Passion and Purpose to Product and Prosperity

Cover design by Nikola Petrovic
Cover photo and headshots by Michael
Pool Photography, Los Angeles

Graphics by Evgeniia Pereplitsa, Russia

Post Hill Press
New York • Nashville
posthillpress.com

Published in the United States of America

1 2 3 4 5 6 7 8 9 10

Table of Contents

❁ INTRODUCTION ❁

If you're picking up this book, it might be because you're a tried-and-true BE... follower. You've devoted your Thursday evenings to experiencing a quantum leap in your life, and you're turning to this first page like you're unboxing a luxuriously wrapped gift. You can't wait to receive the pearls of wisdom from your new friends and mentors Ashley, Korie, and Lisa. You've done the exercises, you're taking the steps, and you're living in a totally different space, having been loved and supported every step of the way. You've challenged yourself to stoke your fire and ignite your passion. You've invented or acquired your products, and you're launching or relaunching with a newfound sense of confidence. Work no longer feels like work. Your business is thriving. You're present and living in abundance.

Or...you have absolutely no idea what we're talking about. And that's not only okay, it's fate. You now have an opportunity to read this book and become part of a movement that's already in motion. We attracted you with our intentions, and you're in exactly the right place. You could be lost in a sea of overwhelming thoughts about the future, or you could be a mega-successful entrepreneur. Doesn't matter. You're here because you want more fulfillment and joy from your life and your business—even if your business is just a twinkle in your eye. We're thrilled you opened this book, and we hope you'll jump in wholeheartedly and trust that the universe is speaking to you. Welcome to the BE... Movement.

If you're new to the BE... Movement, allow us to introduce ourselves.

Ashley Black turned her physical health struggles and near-death experience wisdom into a nine-figure brand. In 2020 she was named as the American Business Association's Entrepreneur of the Year, and she is a number-one bestselling author and TEDx speaker. She invented an award-winning product called the FasciaBlaster® and has been helping millions of users improve their health. She has experienced every facet of business and has now come full circle as she plans her first partial sale and retirement infusion to create balance and peace in her life.

Korie Minkus is the CEO and founder of Rock Your Product®, the number-one, global-product business advisory and growth training company. Korie has mentored, partnered, and designed brand acceleration systems for more than 100,000 emerging and Fortune 500 business owners over the past thirty years. She is an international speaker in consumer psychology and brand leadership, training clients in thirty-two countries. A veteran as a physical-product growth expert, she has launched and scaled hundreds of products, generating more than $1 billion in retail sales. As a global revenue strategist, she delivers outcome-based business solutions and award-winning profit enhancement techniques connecting people, purpose, and product.

Lisa Vrancken is an award-winning TV producer, number-one bestselling author, media expert, and documentary filmmaker with over two decades of expertise as an internationally renowned brand strategist. She crafts commercials and product videos to create brand awareness and drive revenue, providing clients with strategic, full-service video production from start to finish. A globally sought-after product consultant, marketing expert, and public speaker, Lisa has mentored hundreds on their entrepreneurial journeys. With a background in law and human rights advocacy, her mission is to mentor women from all walks of life to stand in their power, while providing them with the tools and frameworks to communicate their truths through the art of visual storytelling.

Through this movement we hope to inspire women to rise and BE...leaders; BE...spiritual as we stand in our power; BE...nurturing as we elevate all women in business; BE... aware so our choices lead to fulfillment; and BE...the change we want to see in the world. In other words, we invite you to embrace your Divine Feminine energy and become who you were always meant to BE...

Now is your moment.

When the three of us decided to collaborate on writing this book, it was because we recognized and valued each other's unique gifts. We felt the presence of the Divine Feminine, uniting us in our collective power. Ladies, if this is the first time you've heard the words Divine Feminine, then we invite you to kick off your heels, unclasp your bra, get comfortable, and prepare yourself for the greatest paradigm shift of your life.

Feminine and masculine energies exist within all of us, regardless of our individual gender. We need both to achieve our full potential, but the world we live in has thrown us far out of balance. For centuries, women have had to suppress our essence. We've learned to compete in a man's world by operating from a place of competitive masculine energy, instead of embracing our cooperative nature. We've scratched and clawed for basic rights. We've fought hard and some of us have become hardened, though we're truly at our most effective in our softness.

The Divine Feminine—your innate wisdom and highest intuition—is awakened when you move through life with trust, love, and faith in your inner self. A long-studied universal frequency, the Divine Feminine is the energy driving our intuition, compassion, collaboration, sensuality, and creativity. In ancient texts, Divine Feminine energy has many names: Shakti (Hinduism), Shekinah (Kabbalah), Yin (Taoism), Prajñāpāramitā (Mahāyāna Buddhism), Gaia/Mother Earth (Wiccan). More recently, the Divine Feminine has been described as the vibration of the Great Goddess: the spiritual mother and ultimate life-giver. Put simply, it's a *vibe*. The Great Goddess vibe.

The Divine Feminine and Divine Masculine may seem like opposite forces, but they're actually complementary and interconnected. True harmony is a balance of introspection and action, intuition and logic, competition and collaboration. When our imagination runs wild, it's reason that grounds us in reality. When we hesitate due to uncertainty, it's courage that emboldens us to push forward. In nature, the petals of the rose are protected by its thorns. Like the rose, our masculine energy allows us to set boundaries, so our feminine is free to bloom. When our energies coexist in harmony, one gives rise to the other. Restoring balance allows all women to step back into our ancient Goddess power.

Many of us have been swept away by modern life, with very little understanding of our true potential. *No more.* We stand on the shoulders of our sisters who came before us. Now is the time to tap into your birthright as a woman, elevate your beautiful Divine Feminine characteristics, and build a successful business and life.

Our book is a celebration of the multitude of energies that we all carry inside of ourselves. It's a call to reconnect with our collective humanity, because we've forgotten our roots. The ebb and flow of the universe is such that the time has come for women to step into our Divine energy and take our proper place as mothers to the world, lovingly holding space as we learn and grow together. We believe this is our rite of passage. Our mission for the book and the BE... Movement is to cast a stone and create ripples so all women can rise.

BE...

BE... was written during one of the shakiest times in global history: the COVID-19 pandemic. It was a year in which three million US women left the labor force—either because they were laid off, or furloughed, or because they made the hard choice to leave their jobs in order to meet the demands of caring for their most vulnerable loved ones and children during mandatory school closings. During this moment, like so many other women, we took a step back to reflect and redesign our lives, our relationships, our state of well-being, and our businesses. The world was, and still is, so unpredictable that only the adaptable will thrive. The only constant is change. We instinctively understood that leaning into change during unprecedented times would require more than a good meditation session, business advisors' meeting, or astrology reading. Real transformation happened within a community of like-minded supporters and a safe space to be accepted, as we began to weave the golden threads of our collective knowledge and experience into what would ultimately become this book.

There's a lot of false promises and posers who prey on the "nice," and no one talks openly about the amount of dishonesty and deception in business. We can't stop this from happening, but we can teach you to "tune in" to that quiet inner voice that says, "No, this is not right for me." Between the three of us, we have acquired over a century of experience in the business world—and we've probably made every mistake in the book. When we embarked on this journey, the intention was to create a road map that would serve to guide and support women in business—along the way it's become something much, much more. We don't want our sisters to step on the same land mines we did, so we've taken the shrapnel and provided the business acumen to help you make confident decisions and to shine a light in all the dark places. We've learned firsthand that the high of success can quickly lead to burnout if we don't stay grounded in our Divine Feminine energy. So, we set out on the path to write a very special business book, just for women. What we didn't expect was for the process to alter us so profoundly.

Statistics show 95 percent of American workers report being stressed at work and 80 percent of people hate their jobs, yet we spend a third of our lives at work. That just sucks. Are you someone, or do you know someone, who spends a huge chunk of time and energy at a job they hate, too strained at the end of the day to do anything else? Oh no, sister, this needs to shift. If you're like many of our followers, you got on the merry-go-round of life at an early age and have been spinning at warp speed ever since. You're taking care of not only your job or business, but also your kids, partners, and parents—sometimes all at the same time—without a moment to breathe, much less design your beautiful life. It's the reality for so many, and we sincerely want to inspire growth for women around the world. The pandemic was the gateway, a shake-up, if you will, forcing all of us to slow our roll and stop the madness. Leap off, ladies, even if you land in the dirt, lose a shoe, and come up cross-eyed—it's time. If you're finally shifting gears to neutral or if you've already ejected, either way, it's a great time to reevaluate and level up.

One amazing thing about the experience of writing this book was the invitation to reflect on our journeys and articulate how we arrived here. For us, it unfolded in a fun and unique way. We formed a private Facebook group, the Writing of the Book (WotB), where we hosted weekly Facebook Live events and opened the writing process to our community. In doing so, we all took part in a critical analysis of the self, which then created exponential opportunities to reveal our true power. We encouraged vulnerability by sharing our deepest truths, connecting with every woman quietly yearning to transform their life. The women in our forum came with open minds, always bringing their A game. As the saying goes: You get back more than you give.

Our Thursday evenings became a give-and-take of energy, climbing to new heights each week as a group. We've not only led the BE... Movement, we've become immersed in it. We've revamped our own lives to be even more purposeful. Like our followers, we've taken new risks, and we're fueled now, more than ever, by our passions. We've created new products and branding for ourselves and mentored and elevated aspiring entrepreneurs, and we're living in prosperity in more tangible and clearly defined ways. We're forever grateful for each other, our sisterhood, and *you*, for sharing this energy. This is our journey so far, and we're just getting started.

After experiencing the inner and outer shifts caused by setting this book into motion, the three of us came together with all the blood, sweat, and tears from years of being engaged in the dynamic world of products. We synthesized our insights, experiences, and expertise as female entrepreneurs into a holistic approach to passion and prosperity. In the chapters to come, we're going to present you with science-based information, both for the inner journey of self-discovery and the creation or expansion of your businesses. Whether you're a stay-at-home mom, corporate leader, product innovator, business owner, service provider, or anything in between, the BE... Movement welcomes you.

The golden threads we weave throughout this book blend concepts from the greatest thinkers of ancient and modern worlds with our own proprietary systems for how to navigate today's business climate. We've done it all—and we have so much to teach you. But this is not a how-to guide: This book won't tell you step-by-step how to patent your product or how to rub elbows with other showstoppers in your field. If that's the sort of information you're looking for, we've got *loads* of resources for you on our social media, and we encourage you to check out our bios in the back of this book. No, this is a book on how to approach the entrepreneurial life. Are you bringing your authentic self to your business? Are you engaging the Divine Feminine on the daily? Are you living your most high-vibrational life? Take our hand. We'll help you.

All entrepreneurs must face failure, and we're no exception. But we've learned that, most often, success in business comes down to one thing: persistence. Persistence isn't a quality that can be faked—but it can be unveiled. Persistence comes from those deepest desires that can get suffocated in the modern world. Believe us, the fire is in there and we are going to light it together. As you read our book, give yourself permission to dig out your passion and your fight so you can carry those qualities into your business. If you tap into what you believe with conviction, you'll be unstoppable. Male narratives of success are common. Our stories, and those of the women we feature in this book, embody what the courage to persist looks and feels like from a woman's perspective. It's time to highlight real-life stories of female entrepreneurship and celebrate the beauty of taking that ancient Goddess vibe into the boardroom and beyond.

In the beginning chapters of this book, you'll discover how to create space in your life to manifest your passions. Through a series of transformational exercises we call "Movements," which you can immediately put into practice, you'll learn to access and channel your inner wisdom. When you're passionate and living purposefully (meaning, in alignment with your true self), the energy will flow. That's what this book is all about: authentically creating your products, business, and beautiful life, while staying grounded in your truth as you move into the deeper waters. We'll provide you with the tools to maintain the staying power you'll need to take your product ideas to market and beyond, and to do that you need to be strong and confident in who you are as a woman. These Movements will serve as a source of understanding and a process of exploration to become more discerning in your decisions. The feeling of being overwhelmed by your responsibilities will dissipate, and the fun of entrepreneurship will surface. This will be a very personal and profound experience.

As you dive deeper into the book, we offer tools that will help you build on your creations and chart your course, no matter what stage you're in. Our book will support you with practical information and thoughtful insights about how the business world really works. Since 2007, the number of female-owned businesses in the US increased by 58 percent—that's more than four times the growth rate of business overall. We can't emphasize enough that you don't need to wait for the perfect idea to join the growing number of female entrepreneurs. The most important thing is to take action. Momentum is key, and we're going to sweep you along like a rushing river. We preach process, not perfection, as the goal. You may read part of the book and decide to keep things simple, or you may decide you're ready to conquer the world. Either way, we're your support system, and we're here to grant you permission to BE...uniquely YOU!

You'll notice as you make your journey through this book that a symbol keeps popping up. It looks like this: When you see this symbol at any point in a given chapter, it should be a reminder to ask yourself what limiting beliefs you might hold around the subject at hand. What fears are you experiencing? What negative self-talk? What do you need to let go of? What do you need to embrace?

So much of the entrepreneurial journey is about knowing what to embrace and what to let go of. And the path is not linear, it's quantum—the universal force of energy in constant motion. And we're not stopping with this book. For the three of us, our purpose in life is to impact the world in a big way through the women we empower. Ours is a ride-till-the-wheels-fall-off attitude. We'll continue to make connections online, showcase our followers, and provide ongoing encouragement to ultimately create a culture of women entrepreneurs, where everyone can experience the support of a solid community. We're here to serve you; as we rise up together, we serve the world.

Our prayer for this book:

We pray with all our hearts for every woman who reads this book. We pray that you guide our hands and our thoughts in the most mindful of ways as we write. We pray for the openness of our readers to accept the wisdom with no judgments and no attachments. We pray that our readers shed limiting beliefs and heal every space in the body that houses them. We pray for lightness to enter the hearts and minds of women; please grant them the creativity and fortitude to invent. We pray for our ladies to take action in their own lives and become the architects of their destinies. We pray for every woman across the globe to be free from oppression and step into expression. We pray for exponential personal, financial, and spiritual growth for every reader. We pray for an elevation in universal consciousness and immediate favor to those who choose to make a difference. Grant each soul permission to experience metamorphosis. Right here, right now, we speak into existence a quantum raising in vibration in every life this book touches. Let every woman radiate passion, purpose, product, and prosperity.

With much love and light,
Ashley Black, Korie Minkus, and Lisa Vrancken

PART I

Passion

❀ CHAPTER ONE ❀

BE… Authentic

LADIES, WELCOME! We can't express enough how happy we are you're embarking on this journey with us. And you're not the only ladies we've been privileged to explore the entrepreneurial path with. At the start of each chapter to come, you'll discover the wise words of women entrepreneurs, many of whom we have had the awesome opportunity to chat with in our WotB (Writing of the Book) social media.

Randi Zuckerberg

To kick off this inaugural chapter on embracing the Divine Feminine (we'll talk more about that in a bit!) and living a life that is authentically YOU, we're bringing in none other than Randi Zuckerberg—yes, that's Mark's sister! Randi is a jack of all trades in her own right: She's a Tony-winning Broadway producer, CEO of Zuckerberg Media, an entrepreneur, investor, tech media personality, former executive at Facebook, and creator of Facebook Live. She's also a beautiful friend who lives her life in accordance with the Divine Feminine, and she is fiercely dedicated to championing other women and girls in STEM fields and business as well. "I think as women we are afraid to take risks because we aren't taught that it's okay to be uncomfortable," Randi says. "From a very young age, boys are told to go outside and play in the dirt. We train boys to be uncomfortable, to be okay with falling down and getting hurt, but we don't raise girls with the same mindset. So, it's not surprising that later in life women takefewer risks in business than men." We love this attitude. If you are to continue reading this book, take note: Transformation into the authentic YOU is not a risk-free process! It takes a lot of hard work and dedication. But it's so worth it to do that work to bring your passionate, authentic self to life. Randi knows this, too. Randi is a superstar of STEM, but she's also got a heart for the arts: "All my life, I wanted to be an actress. That was my dream, and I kept waiting for other people to give me permission, to cast me in their shows, and give me opportunities. Fast forward to when I started my own company, Zuckerberg Media, and created a children's entertainment division to get more girls interested in tech. I had written a children's book called *Dot* that got turned into a television show, and then I got to voice one of the characters. That's when I realized: When you own the casino, you can play in it whenever you want! I had spent my entire life waiting for someone else to give me a part, and all along all I had to do was write the damn show myself." Like Randi discovered, the work, ladies, can't be done by anyone else. YOU must embrace your power and not accept the roles others cast you in (no pun intended!), but pave your own road forward. Strap yourselves in, ladies. The road to your passion, purpose, products, and prosperity awaits you.

twitter.com/randizuckerberg
instagram.com/randizuckerberg

DIVINE FEMININE ENERGY

One of the things we love about Randi's story is that she had so much opportunity and skill in a masculine energy space, but she followed her heart's desire to explore theatre, tapping into her creativity, a very naturally feminine quality. She aligned with her true nature, which is something we will talk a lot about throughout the book.

OK, ladies! Ready to bring out your own inner Goddess for real?

As you've probably guessed from the title of Part I of the book, we're going to kick things off by talking about passion: what it is, how to develop it, and why it's so important in your entrepreneurial life—and your life in general.

But before we can talk about *any* of that, it's important that we cover one of the most important concepts in this book: **Divine Feminine energy**. If you take away nothing else from this book, we hope you'll remember the beautiful characteristics of Divine Feminine energy and how to channel it in your everyday life.

Even if you've never heard of the Divine Feminine, odds are it will seem familiar when we describe it. As we discussed earlier, the Divine Feminine as a concept has been around in some iteration for thousands of years, and almost every culture in the world acknowledges the idea of the feminine energy in one form or another.

But what *is* it? In simple terms, the Divine Feminine is the ultimate maternal energy. She is life-giving, soulful, healing, intuitive, creative, sensitive. She is patient, wise, and gentle. As you've probably guessed from Randi's story, the Divine

Feminine embraces her authentic self and follows her own path, rather than the path society sets out for her. Her energy is tethered to the earth; the Divine Feminine has faith that the earth will provide for her every need.

Now, the Divine *Feminine* presupposes that there is a Divine *Masculine*—and there is! The Divine Masculine embodies such traits as courage, intelligence, sound judgment, independence, strength, and mindfulness. He is the yang to the Divine Feminine's yin. Even though Divine Masculine energy is *masculine*, make no mistake—Divine Masculine energy is not just for men, and in the same way, Divine Feminine energy is not just for women. Everyone, regardless of gender, can live a vibrant, thriving life when they have a healthy balance between their masculine and feminine energies.

But in our patriarchal world, and especially in the realm of business, masculine energy is often the *only* energy we see. In fact, what we often see as "masculine" is not even true masculine energy, but a shadow version of it. This is what we call *hypermasculinity*. Usually, the Divine Masculine and Feminine work against us when there is an energy imbalance. Masculinity becomes hyperactive when traditional masculine qualities like logic, power, or competitiveness sour and are used for selfish purposes: Power and strength become aggression and control; intelligence becomes manipulation; independence becomes coldness or dominance. And when Divine Masculine energy becomes hyperactive, it encourages Divine Feminine energy to become hyperactive as well: The Divine Feminine's patience and gentleness become passiveness and insecurity; her sensitivity becomes victimhood; her healing and support become codependence.

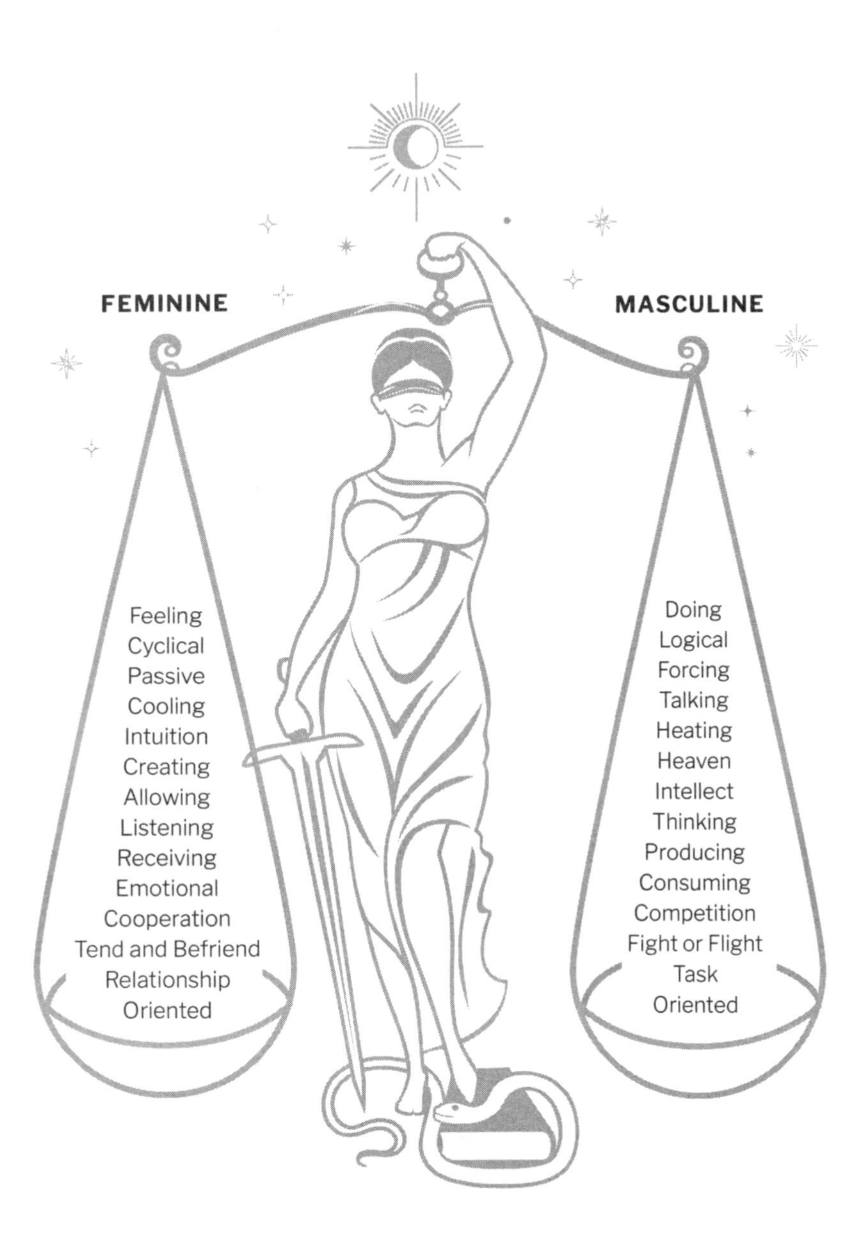
FEMININE
MASCULINE
Feeling
Cyclical
Passive
Cooling
Intuition
Creating
Allowing
Listening
Receiving
Emotional
Cooperation
Tend and Befriend
Relationship
Oriented
Doing
Logical
Forcing
Talking
Heating
Heaven
Intellect
Thinking
Producing
Consuming
Competition
Fight or Flight
Task
Oriented

When a woman desires to evade the "dark side" of her Divine Feminine, she can be pushed too far in the opposite direction and adopt hypermasculine behaviors. This is especially common among female professionals; feminine energy in business is often erroneously viewed as weakness, and thus the stereotype of the hypermasculine female dominates most people's idea of successful female entrepreneurship.

Mimicking masculine business behaviors, independent to a fault, domineering, wily—she will do anything to get ahead, and there is no "end point." She is always fighting for more. She is constantly stressed, working late hours. She is disconnected completely from her Divine Feminine—her true nature.

Let's make this clear: this book is *not* going to tell you how to hack hustle culture. In fact, it's the opposite. We want to deconstruct the idea that the way to succeed in business is to adopt masculine traits. In order to live a life of passion and purpose, we all—no matter our gender—must practice embodying both masculine *and* feminine energies. We want to give the women reading this book the permission to embrace the Goddess within and bring her to center stage, and to flourish in the Divine Feminine.

So, what does all this energy talk have to do with passion? The truth is, there is no direct path to discovering your passion. No magic spell, no mathematical formula to determine what you, our readers, are passionate about.

But...

One thing we know for sure is that passion is inextricably tethered to authenticity, and Divine Feminine energy is *essential* to living authentically. It is only through remembering our soulful, emotional, intuitive side that we begin to know ourselves deeply and begin to discover or amplify our passions—in life, and in our entrepreneurial journey.

Now, maybe that sounds simple enough. Many of you may be rooted in your Divine Feminine and walking in authenticity in your business. For some, this information may be completely new and come from out in left field. Either way, you're in the perfect spot, because we all need a tune-up or a wake-up from time to time. You will view the material in this book from your personal level of consciousness at the time of reading it. So revisiting this book and these Movements at various times in your life could help provide new insights as you evolve. And we will walk you through it all, step by step. So, you may be wondering what the next step is—how you can start channeling your Divine Feminine energy and embody your most authentic self.

That's where the science of brain waves comes in....

BRAIN WAVES

Passion is your authentic self connecting with your actions. Purpose is tying those actions to the greater good. Sounds simple enough, yet so many of us lack passion and purpose in our daily lives. We're grinding through on autopilot, disconnected and out of sync with the Divine Feminine. We call this "Time to Make the Donuts" mode.

Some of you may remember the popular 1980s TV ad campaign featuring Dunkin' Donuts's sleep-deprived mascot, Fred the Baker. "Time to make the donuts" is the phrase he repeated over and over in a lifeless monotone as he jolted awake before dawn, stumbled to the bathroom in his jammies, drove to work in the dark, baked all day, and then drove home from the grind in the dark again, muttering, "I made the donuts." Even though the Fred campaign was wildly successful and presented as Fred's commitment to his work, we thought it was a funny and memorable way to describe this mode of beta functioning.

Many of us can relate to Fred: He's stuck on the hamster wheel of life, going through the motions day after day. His energy is imbalanced, he's not present or mindful, and he's void of passion and purpose. Take a few minutes and reflect on whether you may be living in a Time to Make the Donuts state of mind. Are you sleepwalking through each day in a fog? Slogging through meetings, answering emails, making meals, doing laundry, and helping with homework before finally collapsing on the couch with a glass of wine and a Netflix series, completely exhausted? Time to Make the Donuts mode feels comfortable—even safe—but it's also a sign that we've become locked into fixed habits. If we want to develop our passions and lead a purposeful life, it isn't going to happen in Time to Make the Donuts mode.

"As a high-paid, high-stress executive for twenty-five years, and a working mom (oh and a wife, friend, and sister), I was stuck on the hamster wheel. It became obvious as I took my frustration out on my marriage and made excuses to avoid friends because I did not want to face my reality. I lost my free spirit and creative thinking, and I always gave and never dreamed of receiving. I became only logical and linear. It was my own fault. I fell prey to Time to Make the Donuts. Until one day five years ago, I chose to redefine my talent as innovative, listen to my intuition, forgive, reflect, receive, and design a more aligned self."

K

Korie Minkus

Research suggests adults spend the majority of their time exercising their beta brain waves. These are the brain waves that we use to hammer out tasks. Beta in and of itself is not bad, unless it's wayyyyyy out of balance. When beta gets out of balance, you can get stuck in Time to Make the Donuts mode, which is a sign of trouble. So how do we get off the hamster wheel of life? Our daily schedule and our ingrained habits and beliefs can seem so inflexible. But one of the biggest myths is that the brain we have now is the brain we'll always have—that the habits and beliefs we have cultivated since birth are here to stay.

> *"Many years ago, I saw the potential to make big bucks fast. I took a role as a US distributor of a non-invasive anti-aging device for the east coast. I took the exclusivity. I sold my soul for the almighty dollar. It wasn't my passion. I spent tireless hours selling, day after day. I followed the material world instead of my own personal vision of my soul's passion. So, I bowed out to do what I love: telling stories through visual media."*
>
> **L**
>
> **Lisa Vrancken**

We're here to tell you you *can* transform your life, you *can* shake yourself out of Time to Make the Donuts mode. Science backs us up: According to neuroscientist Joe Dispenza, every time we learn a new thing, our brain *literally* rewires itself. Every time we perform a new action, feel a new feeling, or think a new thought, we create a new neural pathway. Habits are just well-travelled neural pathways, and just like a well-worn path in a forest, if abandoned long enough, they will start to disappear. This ability for the brain to develop new neural pathways is called *neuroplasticity*. In this book, we're not going to preach to you about changing your life, we're going to invite you to do some simple things to promote neuroplasticity and bring about new brain waves that spark passion and purpose.

CREATE NEW **THOUGHT** PATTERNS

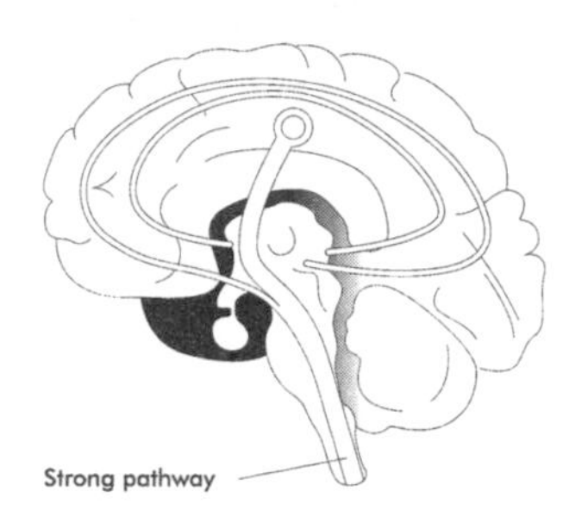

PATHWAYS

Pathways connect areas of the brain. Each route the neurological impulse travels is associated with behavior

When we have a thought (especially with a heightened emotion) we reinforce the path. Call this a "habit" and the brain loves this habitual path of least resistance

---

NEUROPLASTICITY

New thoughts create new paths

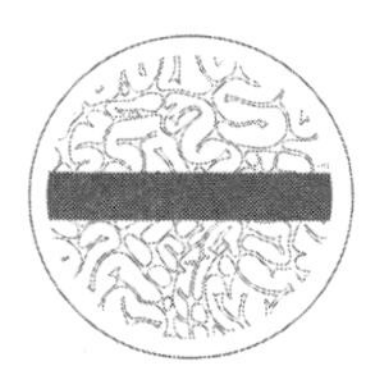

Practice strengthens path

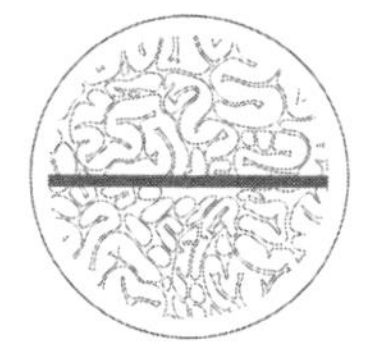

Old thoughts weaken

We have to "be it to become it" and take control of our thoughts until they carve new "grooves in the record"

The first step to rewiring our brains and engaging with the Divine Feminine is becoming aware of how our brains operate in the first place. We are not claiming to be brain scientists, but we do think it's important to touch on some of the basics. First of all, the human brain is constituted of billions of specialized cells called *neurons*, and these neurons are in constant communication with one another. The bursts of electrical activity produced by the neurons' "conversations" are called brain waves. Brain waves were first discovered by neuroscientist Hans Berger in the 1920s, when he performed the very first electroencephalogram—that is, a recording of the electrical waves present in the brain (also known as an EEG). As you can probably imagine, understanding your brain waves is pretty important to living a healthy and authentic life.

There are five types of brain waves: **gamma**, **beta**, **alpha**, **theta**, and **delta**. They vary in frequency, and each brain wave is linked to a different level of consciousness or cognitive processing. **Gamma** waves, the highest frequency, are generated during expanded consciousness and peak focus (e.g., meditation). Gamma waves develop in adulthood. Next on the frequency scale are **beta** waves, which develop between the ages of eight and twelve and allow us to concentrate on day-to-day tasks. These are the brain waves we emit when we're focused on activities like driving, scrolling social media, answering emails, or staying engaged in Zoom meetings. Beta is necessary, but we don't want it to be all-consuming and lead to Time to Make the Donuts energy. Just below beta are **alpha** waves, which develop between the ages of five to eight.

This is the frequency we produce when we shift into a relaxed or reflective state—e.g., when we brainstorm, paint, compose music, or are in mad scientist mode. Alpha is a childlike mindset, where our outer world of fantasy and imagination blends with our inner world of intuition; you might consider it a bridge from our external world (gamma, beta) to our internal world (theta, delta). Alpha is an energetic frequency that will be vital as we unearth our passions. Lastly, the lowest frequency waves on the scale are **theta** (a dreaming or trance-like state) and **delta** (produced during deep, restorative sleep). Both of these kinds of brain waves develop between birth and four years of age.

Ever been hypnotized? If not, I'm sure you've seen characters on TV hypnotize people by swinging a pocket watch back and forth, back and forth, back and forth in front of their face and asking, "Are you getting sleeeeeepy?" That's brain waves in action, baby! When you undergo hypnosis, the hypnotist activates your theta brain waves to make your thoughts more malleable. So while many of your habits and beliefs are formed in childhood, it's possible to reshape them—even well into adulthood—by engaging the right brain waves, like theta (more on that later!). While delta is important for getting a good night's sleep, studies indicate, alarmingly, that many people are actually walking around in delta mode during the day! If you sleepwalk your way through the day, do you know what that makes you? That makes you a *Zombie*, girl!

"The WotB, our community's LIVE weekly podcast on Facebook, gained momentum with new members seeking a contemporary room of females seeking elevation, ascension, and up-to-date ways of being. We created a place to explore alpha waves, and whether a mom, corporate warrior, visionary, or business entrepreneur, we welcome all women into this private group. Weekly, we talk on subjects that challenge your everyday routine, expand your thought process, and bring freshness to your approach. We interview experts across passion, purpose, business, and prosperity. This mind-expanding and supportive experience is absolutely FREE. Our ethos and mission is to collaborate, share, draw new bonds within and collectively, and build together. It takes a village, and doing it with like-minded women is simply more fun."

K

Korie Minkus

So how do we overcome being a "Zombie," or eking out our existence in Time to Make the Donuts mode? Well, the answer isn't to stop activating our beta and delta brain waves. Just as we all must balance masculine and feminine energies, there is a time and place for every type of brain wave; however, it's important when walking the path of your highest and best life to maintain balance among all of them. By bringing awareness to the brain waves you're exhibiting throughout the day, you put yourself in a better position to exponentially improve your daily habits as necessary to become healthier, more expansive, and more authentic so that you can start living your most kickass life!

"I live by the motto: health from the inside out. As a competitive figure skater, I effectively use exercise to channel my alpha waves formed from childhood. From the age of four, when I stepped on the ice, movement designed my meditative state and happy place, allowing mindful relaxation to create. Today, I remain dedicated to maintaining vitality and energy. To activate my alpha brain waves, I engage in holistic health practices, regulate proper hydration, incorporate movement into my day, and make conscious food and lifestyle choices. These activities help me to maintain focus, elevated flow, and generate productive solutions to tackle life's greatest opportunities. And there was never a more freeing time in my life than when I put on my feminine sequence costumes, freshly sharpened skates, and glided over the smooth ice. Talking about flow!"

Korie Minkus

Make no mistake, identifying the brain waves you're engaging isn't a black-and-white matter, as many activities harness more than one type of brain wave or promote other brain waves—exercising is not only a means of engaging your beta brain waves, it can also put you into a trancelike delta state, and the creativity and confidence necessary to engage your alpha mode is frequently boosted through accomplishing ego-boosting beta tasks. Also keep in mind that different people don't always engage the same brain wave via the same activity; for instance, reading might be a great way to get your alpha waves flowing, but for someone else, it's a chore that throws them in beta mode. Different strokes! When you pay attention to the brain waves you're engaging in throughout the day and recognize what activates them, you can break out of a Zombie or Time to Make the Donuts life and tap into a life of passion and purpose.

As we said above, the brain wave we want to lean into as we work to unearth our passions is alpha. Alpha mode is the sweet spot between extreme consciousness (gamma) and pure rest (delta). Think back to when you were a kid, and the world was your oyster. What did you do with your time? Coloring, playing, reading, making discoveries, annoying the bejesus out of your parents with your constant questions! You might be able to see why this brain wave lends itself to discovering passion: the ability to play, freely and *without judgment*, is the key to becoming passionate. It's the key to pulling us out of Zombie mode, which has us numb to life, like the living dead, and Time to Make the Donuts mode, which has us moving through the world on autopilot, like a robot.

High Spirituality And Connectedness
GAMMA
Time To Make The Doughnuts
BETA
Creative And Recharging
ALPHA
Dreamy And Reprogramming
THETA
Deep Sleep
DELTA

"Back in the earlier days of my business I would grind away in Time to Make the Donuts mode, feeling guilty if all my time and energy weren't devoted to plowing forward towards success. Then I would burn myself out and bail and go surfing. While 'taking time off to surf' I inevitably came up with ideas that I would bring back to the business with new life. It became a joke with my employees that I needed to go surf. And I did. Surfing is a wonderful alpha waves activity for me. I'm totally present, totally connected to nature, and free of stressful thoughts, and my brain is cracked open for my innate creativity. Then the answers come to me! Now surfing and other alpha-waves activities like gardening and decorating are a regular part of my daily life. My alpha waves are intentional and mindful and, most importantly, prioritized."

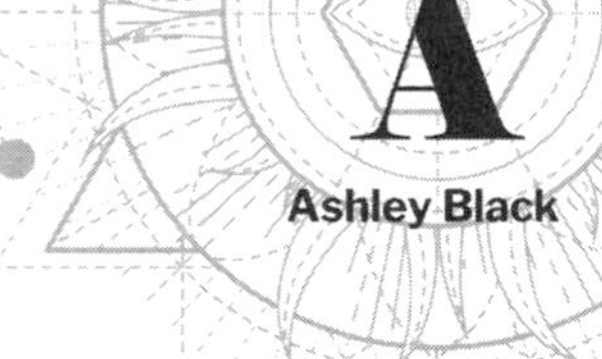

Ashley Black

But though alpha mode represents a childlike state, you don't need to be a kid to rev your alpha engine; in fact, as an adult you can (and we suggest you do) engage in alpha mode often. There are quick tricks to alter your brain waves (we call this "biohacking"). These can include listening to binaural beats (Spotify is full of great binaural playlists targeted to specific brain waves) and, if you have the means, working with a neurofeedback coach, who will perform an EEG to identify which brain waves you're currently engaging in and help you to change them. You can supercharge your alpha brain waves specifically by listening to alpha binaural beats or by engaging in activities that excite the playful or creative part of you, like surfing, dancing, or meeting a new person.

It's also helpful to take a good hard look at just *where* your time and energy are going throughout the day—are you engaging in Time to Make the Donuts mode from dawn till dusk? Are you slogging through the workday like a Zombie? Or are you getting time to breathe and create and just *BE*? Is the life you want to be living matching up with the life you *are* living?

To help you answer these questions, we've created a Movement inviting you to assess which brain waves you're engaging throughout your day. Behold, the Brain Wave Balancing Act!

MOVEMENT #1: BRAIN WAVE BALANCING ACT

For this Movement, we invite you to consider when, throughout your day, you engage the different brain waves. Is your day job really just nine straight hours of beta mode? Are you getting solid sleep at night that gets your delta waves flowing? Maybe a weekly or daily yoga practice could serve you a much-needed dose of gamma waves! Understanding what waves you're engaging in throughout the day can help you figure out how to organize your time to make you a happier, healthier, and more Divinely Feminine version of yourself!

As you may have noticed, identifying activities that correspond to specific brain waves can be a challenge—especially since many activities engage more than one brain wave, and not everyone activates their brain waves via the same activities! But we've compiled a list of activities that are generally associated with specific brain waves, beginning with gamma, the most external brain wave, and ending with delta, the most internal.

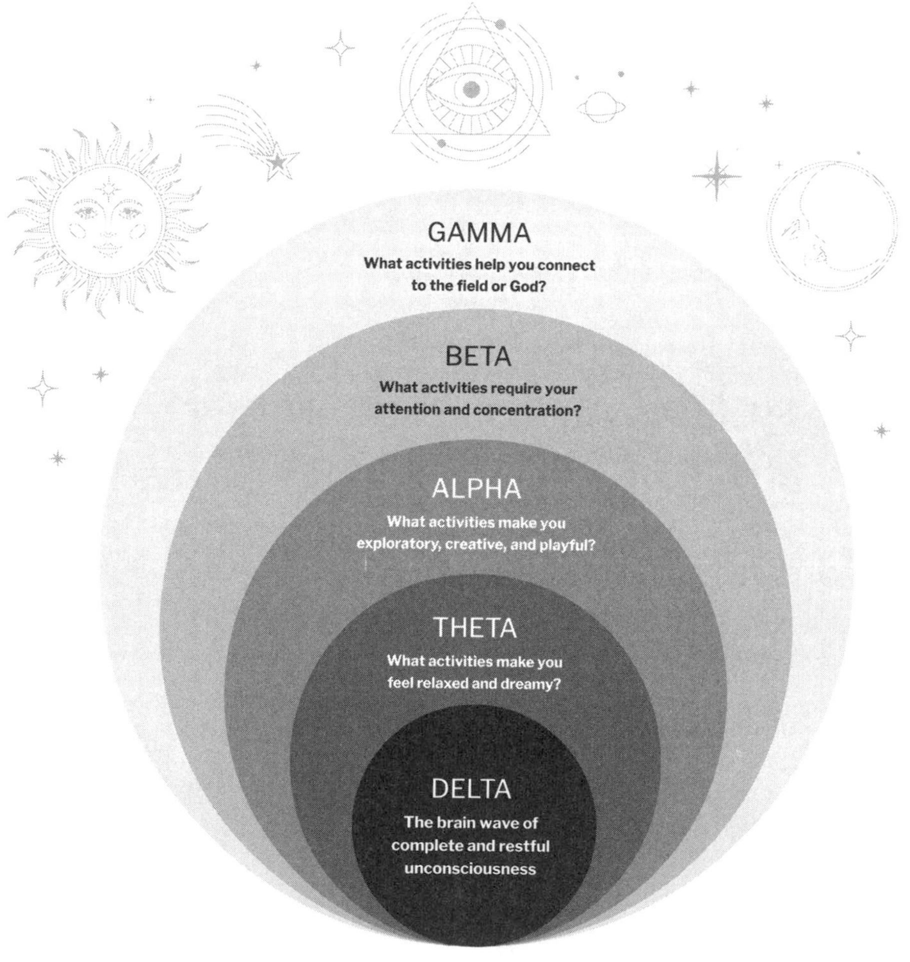

- Gamma: What activities help you connect to the field or God? You might try activities like meditation, walking in nature, praying (connecting to Gamma requires letting go of stress and trauma to tap into these ascended brain waves)
- Beta: What activities require your attention and concentration on the external world? Beta is usually present in our day-to-day activities like working on the computer, paying bills, or driving. (Be aware of spending too much time in Beta)
- Alpha: What activities make you exploratory, creative, and playful? You might try art, writing, making music, exploratory cooking, dancing, playing a sport, talking to a new person... (We need to strategically make time for more of these activities in our lives)
- Theta: What activities make you feel relaxed and dreamy? You might try hypnotism, sound journeys, guided meditation or active meditation, soaking in a tub...(This is where we can go to shift limiting beliefs)
- Delta: The brain wave of complete and restful unconsciousness, most often seen in deep, dreamless sleep (We need to be conscious of the need for 7-9 hours a night to detox, and sleeping during dark hours)

You might notice some activities transcend brain waves. This is because, while performing a specific activity *can* jump-start a specific brain wave, *how* you approach the activity also has an effect on what brain waves are being used. For example, maybe painting engages your creative alpha flow—or maybe illustration is your day job, and you've fallen into a Time to Make the Donuts beta slog (if this describes you, we'll talk about how to apply more meaning to your daily life in the next section of this book!). Or maybe, as we've already said, an activity that works for one person simply doesn't work for you—to each their own! The key to balancing your brain waves isn't to follow our chart to the letter, or to follow what anyone else is doing, but to see what activities work for *you* and give you the most balance.

So think about your daily life and the brain waves you find yourself operating in the most. Are you a Donut Maker? Are you a Zombie? How do you think you might shake up your world a little so that your brain waves will all operate in balance with one another, promoting a life of Divine Feminine zen?

"I am turning fifty, and I vividly remember about three or four years ago saying to myself, 'I want the second half of my life to be even better than the first,' and I made a commitment to myself to seek how to remove all blockages and become limitless. I read books, I did retreats, I addressed past traumas—I really dove headfirst into understanding how I could create the life of my dreams.

So much of it turned out to be balancing the brain, which balances the body and the emotions and, ultimately, the life. I had a desire to achieve high gamma, where I believe we tap into Universal wisdom, but I was trapped in an addiction to the stress chemicals of Time to Make the Donuts. I began to intentionally practice different brain states, and my brain began to balance. Now, getting into meditation and achieving high gamma happens often, but it really was and is still a journey of hour-by-hour, intentional balancing of my brain waves. You have an 'in-the-moment choice,' ladies, to shift; you just have to decide it's important—and it is."

A

Ashley Black

Movement #1 Brain Wave Balancing Act

Brainwave	What are some activities I do in this mode?	How do I reflect my Divine Feminine Energy when in this mode?	How do I feel when I spend time in this mode?	Do I need more of this brain wave? Less? What can I do to achieve brain wave balance?
Gamma				
Beta				
Alpha				
Theta				
Delta				

"As women, we share an inner knowing. It's a special kind of intuition—it's our divine power. When we expand our horizons through healing and self-awareness, we create the kind of prosperity that becomes a life force in itself. The saying 'behind every successful woman is a tribe of other successful women that have her back' is as true now as ever. We all want to live a life that sets our souls on fire, and it's possible for each and every one of us. It takes both individual work and community support to write the story that is your life. We share the message with women around the globe: By coming together and amplifying our voices, we transform our experiences into personal power, profound meaning, and prosperous spirit. My loving words of wisdom for anyone seeking the next step on their path: 'On your own journey of discovery, touch as many souls, uplift as many lives, and make a positive impact on as many people as possible.'"

L

Lisa Vrancken

For your consideration

FOR YOUR CONSIDERATION: Take a few moments to reflect on the work you just did for this Movement. Look at the words you just wrote. What three words that you have added to the chart above ignite your passion the most? Write them here:		
1.	2.	3.

❀ CHAPTER TWO ❀

BE...
High-Vibrational

Natasha Graziano

Influencer and motivational speaker Natasha Graziano has been making waves on Instagram and Clubhouse for the last few years. At thirty-one, Natasha has 7.5 million Instagram followers (and counting), is a number-one bestselling author, and has been named the number-one female motivational speaker under forty—which isn't surprising! When Natasha speaks, she resonates at a frequency that others want to bathe in. We LOVE her dedication and energy to manifestation, so we invited her to speak with us in the WotB, where she let us in on her secret to success: the five pillars of success—her tools for overcoming difficulty and achieving her dreams!" Pillar number one: Get clarity on your vision. Write down your statement. And know *exactly*what it is you want.... Write it down. That way, your subconscious mind finds a wayto try to bring this to fruition faster. Pillar number two: Remove the blockages. Remove the self-limiting beliefs...." (We'll talk more about self-limiting beliefs in a few chapters!) "Pillar three: Replace old self-limiting beliefs with new positive beliefs.... Pillar number four is *expand your vision.* So

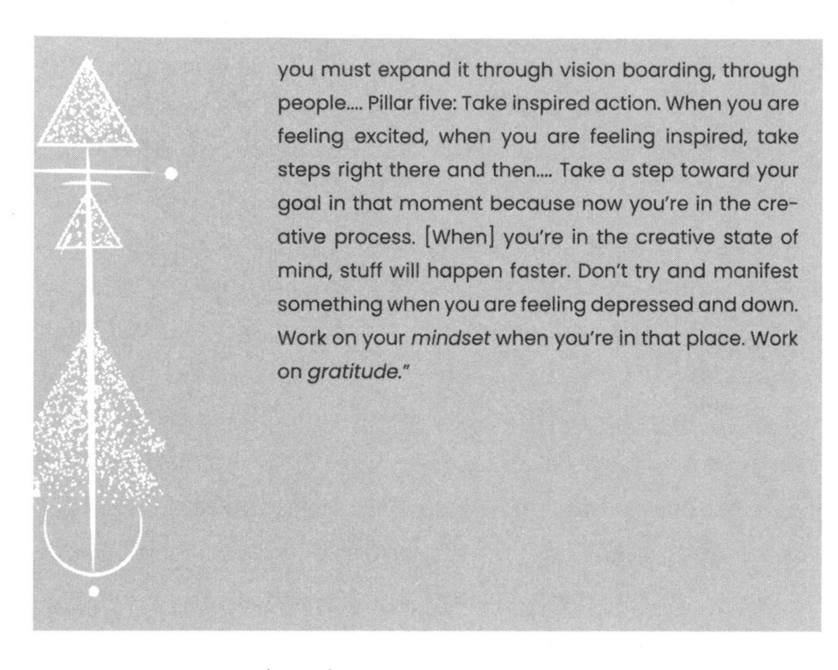

you must expand it through vision boarding, through people.... Pillar five: Take inspired action. When you are feeling excited, when you are feeling inspired, take steps right there and then.... Take a step toward your goal in that moment because now you're in the creative process. [When] you're in the creative state of mind, stuff will happen faster. Don't try and manifest something when you are feeling depressed and down. Work on your *mindset* when you're in that place. Work on *gratitude*."

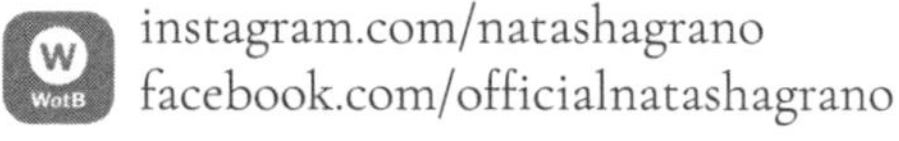

instagram.com/natashagrano
facebook.com/officialnatashagrano

HIGH VIBRATION AND LOW VIBRATION

We embrace Natasha's art of manifestation, and we want to see all of you achieve your dreams just like she has. When we said she resonates at a frequency others gravitate toward, we weren't speaking metaphorically. Did you know that each person operates on their own vibrational level? We're not just talking about "vibes," we're talking about something tangible and measurable. This vibration can transmit into the quantum field and affect not only you, but everyone around you. The old saying goes, "You can't help others until you help yourself," but we are going to modernize that by saying "You can't raise the vibration of others or the planet until you raise your own vibration." You can raise your vibration so high that it becomes an internal state, free from influence by the external world. This takes practice and consistency, but we are going to show you exactly how you can do that.

Let's first visit what high vibration and low vibration *feel* like. When you feel anxious, shameful, or guilty, that is a sign you're operating at a **low level of vibration**—that the parasitic energies with which you're engaging internally and possibly externally are depleting your passion and purpose. Guilt is a low-vibrational energy for everyone, but wouldn't you know it, according to recent studies, women tend to feel excessive guilt in their day-to-day lives—especially compared to men. According to an article published by NBC titled "Women guilty of feeling too guilty, study shows," studies also indicate that men don't feel *enough* guilt. (Can ladies ever get a break?!) Alternatively, when you feel peace, love, compassion, you're operating at a **high level of vibration**, meaning the energies with which you're engaging are boosting you up and giving you a sense of purpose.

Pop quiz: Which level of vibration would you rather have?

If you answered "high vibration"—you're spot on! High-vibrational living is a life that most people can't even imagine. A heaven on earth, so to speak. If you answered "low vibration"—we have some things to work on! And if you answered, "*Huh?*" then maybe we ought to back up a little.

Nikola Tesla purportedly said, "If you want to understand the universe, you must think in terms of energy, frequency, and vibration." Energy is *everywhere*. It's in our food, it's in our friendships, it's in our cars and in the drivers in the other cars, it's in the forest, it's in the gym, it's in our workspaces. It's in the family photos and the succulents that we use to brighten up our environment. And it's in *us*. And the energy we surround ourselves with has a *huge* effect on our health and wellness.

Science tells us that our bodies are, in fact, vibrating bundles of electromagnetic energy, and that those bundles of energy are constantly interacting with the energies of everything else. Your entire body, down to the smallest cell in your pinky toe, is vibrating, and your overall wellbeing is constituted of the sum energy of all your cells: high-vibrating cells means an overall high-vibrational energy, and low-vibrating cells means an overall low-vibrational energy. And the higher your vibration, the healthier your cells are and the more passionate and purposeful you can be.

Pretty cool, huh? It gets even cooler: scientists have discovered that the human heart emits an electromagnetic field that extends about eight feet from the body, and that electromagnetic field both attracts and gives off energy. So when we talk about people being in our "personal bubbles," it's actually true! Like tuning forks, we respond to the vibrations around us. Tuning forks try to match frequencies, so it works both ways. You can "spread your light" and affect the vibration of others or the environment, or a negative place, person, scenario can affect yours. Basically, all energies, vibrations, and frequencies are interconnected. It's a very cool way to view the world and the way we fit into it. In this chapter, we're going to teach you to calibrate your tuning fork so you can protect your energy and raise your vibration.

Dr. David Hawkins studies the science of vibration and consciousness, and he created the point system you see here to gauge different levels of vibration. High-energy vibrations are associated with feelings of love, enlightenment, joy, and peace—all the emotions necessary to expand your consciousness so that you can cultivate passion and purpose. Meanwhile, low-energy vibrations are associated with sadness, purposelessness, shame, anger, and restlessness—all emotions that leave you closed-off and unable to live with passion. And your energy is inextricably connected to your ability to balance your Divine Masculine and Feminine energies; like we said, guilt, which is one of the lowest-vibrational emotions, is hugely common among women as compared to their male counterparts. But guilt is actually the "shadow" emotion of empathy, which is a major feminine attribute! In short, when you fearlessly balance your Masculine and Feminine energies, your vibration level goes up, too.

So it turns out, when the Beach Boys sang, "I'm picking up good vibrations," they were being literal! But according to Dr. Hawkins, most people spend their lives at around 204. Two hundred four! As he says, "All levels below 200 are destructive of life in both the individual and society at large." This is serious business! Can you imagine how incredible the world would be if everyone were operating at 1000? There is so much smack talk out there right now about being high-vibrational, but how do we accomplish this in the real world? We've said it before, we'll say it again: The first step to elevating your life is to become aware of what you WANT to elevate! You can't raise your vibration levels without scuffing off the things that lower your vibration in the first place.

"As an active and seasoned professional (corporate-trained) perfectionist, letting go has meant accepting the parts of me that I define as 'not-so-perfect.' It started when my older son was ten years old, and I went to see a therapist because I was concerned with his inability to go to sleep at night. The therapist (Bob—who I adore till this day) told me it was not my son that was messed up, but it was me! He began to help me unravel the layers to accept the parts of me that I was trying to hide. I discovered how truly responsible I was for setting my own boundaries and attracting negativity, fear, and pain. Surrounded with dominant male figures in my personal and professional life and a highly sterile corporate setting for almost three decades, I made choices to minimize myself. Often as the only woman at the boardroom table, I downplayed the high vibration that defined me, as my animation and passion was not always appreciated. When I became aware of my subconscious pattern, I chose to shift to attract more like-minded high vibration individuals, ignite a newfound energy, and raise my body's frequency to create game-changing outcomes personally and professionally. The journey continues daily, and the work is never done. But awareness and conscious choices have been the key."

K

Korie Minkus

MEGAHERTZ OF EMOTIONS

A chart by David Hawkins, MD, PhD
Our emotions create a literal vibration and that vibration sets off a chemical chain reaction in the body.

LEVEL		EMOTION
Enlightenment	700-1000	Ineffable
Peace	600	Bliss
Joy	540	Serenity
Love	500	Reverance
Reason	400	Understanding
Acceptance	350	Forgiveness
Willingness	310	Optimism
Neutrality	250	Trust
Courage	200	Affirmation
Pride	175	Scorn
Anger	150	Hate
Desire	125	Craving
Fear	100	Anxiety
Apathy	50	Despair
Guilt	30	Blame
Shame	20	Humiliation

Source: David R. Hawkins, M.D., Ph.D., Power vs. Source: *The Hidden Determinants of Human Behavior* (Carlsbad, CA: Hay House, Inc., 2014).

We've devised the Five Circles of High-Vibrational Living to provide a tangible way for you to elevate your vibration across the board.

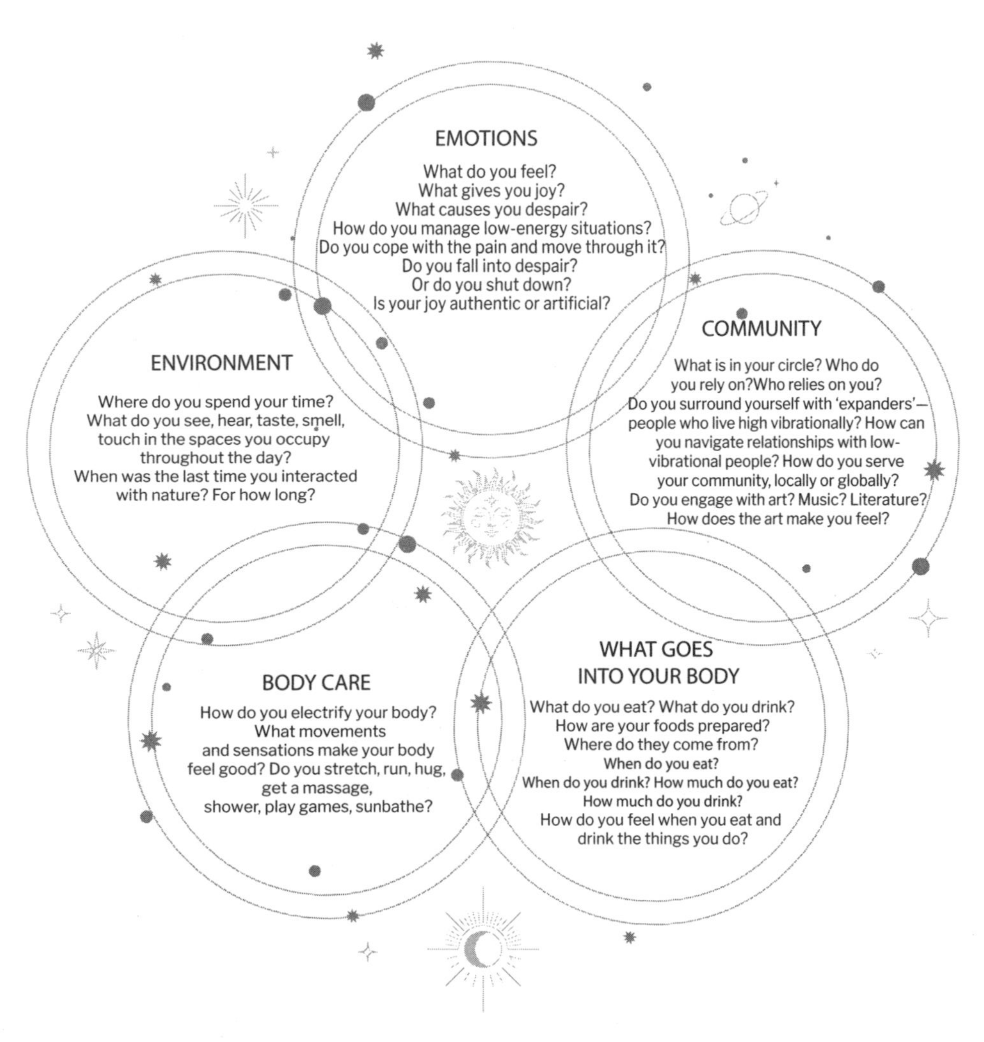

Each circle pertains to a different arena of your everyday life: your **environment**, your **emotions**, **what you put in your body**, **body care**, and **community**.

When you consider your **environment**, consider any of the physical locations where you spend time: your office, your home, your school, your place of worship, your local park, your community garden. How do you feel in these places? Pay attention. What do you need to let go of?

You need to feel good in your spaces. Remember the "vibe" of the environment is like that tuning fork. Is it elevating your vibration, or working against you? You can improve your environment by doing something as simple as deep-cleaning your home or office and bringing some candles, flowers, and crystals. Or you could be more dramatic and move to the beach. What we are saying is, have awareness and intentionally spend your time in high-vibrational environments.

Your **emotions** refers to just that—how you feel! The goal of high-vibrational living isn't to be *Whoo hooo, life is the best, let's be happy!* If you refer back to the science of emotions, the highest-vibrational feeling, behind enlightenment, is peace and bliss at 600MHz. And the best part? Peace is something we can create. Living high-vibrationally means creating that peace for yourself. But the last thing we want is to equate passionate and purposeful living with bottling up "negative" emotions or putting on a happy mask! The only way to be at peace is to feel those "negative" feelings when they come—and shift to practice gratitude!

We can learn to guide our emotions just by paying attention to them, accepting them, and learning to manage them. We can raise our vibrational emotional energy intentionally.

Think about your emotional energy. What do you need to let go of here? What can you replace it with?

"As a lover of both travel and time spent in study, with Spirit, or in solitude, I've learned the art of identifying and creating sacred spaces. Whether I'm on the go producing videos or spending time in my guesthouse nestled near the beach in the Sunshine State, I always take a moment to assess the energetic qualities of a room or place.

Throughout my life, I've brought heart, healing, and restoration into spaces where negativity was occurring. In the early years, I was exposed to a lot of tension and difficult energies in my home. I've felt intuitively called to reinvigorate environments. In my thirties, I took a worn-down home from a state of disrepair to a state of reinvention, and I did the same with myself. It was in the walls of this house, which started out as forgotten bones, that I created a space of focused, powerful learning. I worked on revitalizing the aging structure during the day. At night, I dove into the study of the power of the mind. I avidly read books on everything from major religions to quantum physics, becoming well-versed in meditation and mindfulness practices. I received certifications in biofeedback, neuro-linguistic programming, and hypnotherapy, which ultimately played a big role in reprogramming my own daily brain waves and early emotional imprints, and now I'd like to share it with the world!"

Lisa Vrancken

"I'm not afraid to say that I faced some dysfunction early on, which led to a lot of powerfully charged emotions. The first thing to recognize is that, as humans, we're going to experience every emotion on the spectrum. I highlight the importance of embracing everything about your journey; it's made you who you are. Shame is rooted in the fear that something you perceive as making you less worthy is going to be uncovered or found out by your peers. And yet, the truth is that a long road filled with twists and turns and the occasional dark alley doesn't make you any less valuable. You are inherently worthy in your humanity, because of the fact that you have a soul and a spirit and a purpose. Do not be ashamed of your negative emotions; instead, make space to heal. It's your duty to revel in everything the world has to offer, integrating the harder lessons and focusing on the warmth of shared laughter and the sweetest pleasures of life."

Lisa Vrancken

"Growing up in a family circle that continually was intellectually stimulating, I became aware I thrive in a state of being challenged and linear thinking. I seek provoking ideas, love difficult situations, am extremely methodical, and create my best work as a rational problem solver. However, I discovered a sabotage pattern in my life with emotional low energy when I was not intellectually challenged. Sometimes it's about letting go, however more often it's about replacing a bad habit with a more productive one. This awareness allowed me to discover new pleasures around challenge. I have applied a more lateral experience to life, thinking more outside the box. For me, I discovered a charged emotional state when I let myself get messy (wear my hair frizz-curly), random thinking (stop what I am doing to write a friend a deep loving message), and spontaneity (jumping on my bike and just riding as far as my body will take me), all to provoke a new sense of challenge. Aha!!"

K

Korie Minkus

What you put in your body means what you eat, drink, and otherwise take in, but you don't have to be extreme, just mindful. We can personally attest that some of us enjoy a glass of red wine at the end of a long day, or a decadent piece of cake for dessert! But being high-vibrational means being mindful of how what you take in makes you feel.

> *"I used to believe indulgence was all about living life to the fullest. I've enjoyed many kinds of delicious vices, from caffeine and cigarettes to rich French foods and a glass of Veuve Clicquot! For a long time, nothing could stop me...until the party finally came to a halt in May 2011. I went into the hospital to have my appendix removed. While I was undergoing tests, doctors found a grapefruit-sized tumor between my heart and lung. The biopsy confirmed it was Hodgkin's lymphoma. It rocked my world, and for the first time, I had the realization that I wasn't invincible. I needed to change my lifestyle, ASAP. My cousin Niki gifted me with wellness warrior Kris Carr's* Crazy Sexy Cancer *books, where I learned different healing modalities with a spotlight on nutrition. I've been in remission ever since."*

You probably remember learning about the food pyramid in grade school. Well, we want to introduce you to the food pyramid of high-vibrational living:

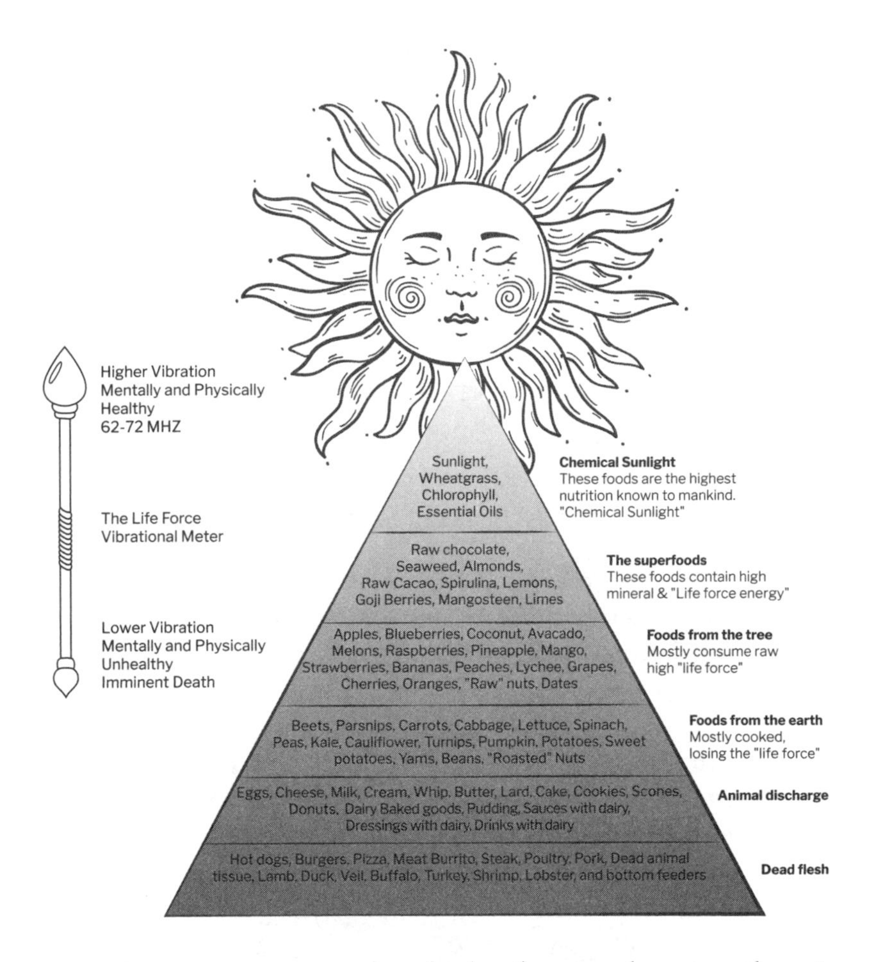

We want to stress that high-vibrational eating doesn't require any extreme behaviors. High-vibrational living is about giving your body what it needs to be strong and energized—including sunlight, the highest source of nutrition. So, what food energizes you? Are you losing control when you eat, or are you aware of what you're putting into your body? If you'd like to better understand how to eat more high-vibrationally, we recommend the chart above to raise your awareness. Remember ladies, as the old saying goes, "everything in moderation."

"For me, as a young athlete, diet and food has always been a source of focus and importance in my life. However, when I turned forty years old, I began to have chronic migraines and then, a skin reaction that caused an awful rash on my face. I discovered through some blood work and an ANA test that my immune system was attacking my body. With health being a continuum of priority, this took me by great surprise. Doctors were quick to offer Western drugs to resolve my challenges but I rejected the notion of modern medicine to find the solution. I began to research my diet, and my best friend recommended a book called Eat Right for Your Type *by Dr. Peter J. D'Adamo, which taught me about the chemistry of your blood and introduced me to the Blood Type Diet. I discovered how I was sabotaging my health efforts. Strangely, eating tomatoes, corn, and avocados may sound healthy for some, but it does not jive with my blood type as a blood type B. Committed to this change of life, and a diet for better health outcomes, I was able to 100 percent reverse the damage and go on to test negative for ANA. To this day, I am a HUGE believer in the Blood Type Diet and how it's designed to eliminate the main source of inflammation we self-impose on our bodies daily."*

K

Korie Minkus

So think about what you put in your body. What do you need to let go of? What might you replace it with?

Physical energy refers not just to hard exercise—though it can! It refers to energy the body likes, which includes movement that electrifies the body, but it also includes, well, sitting still! Yoga, sex, relaxing in the sauna, getting a massage, sunbathing, laughing, lying in the grass.

"I have always had a fascination with the warmth and glow of the sun. Growing up in Chicago, where we only get 50 percent of our year in sunshine cover, I get very easily deprived of sunlight. You may know this already, but science be told, a sunny day increases levels of the natural mood-lifting chemical serotonin. So, I have become obsessed with being in the sun. For both mental health and the generation of vitamin D, a key disease-preventing health benefit. In fact, this may be unpopular, but I do not subscribe to sunscreen and I believe the sun has natural healing properties that should not need a barrier. I am careful about my exposure in the sun, and I do cover up to keep from burning; however, I am a huge subscriber to the value our sun has on our personal elevation of physical energy. Find me happiest at a beach, on a boat, or on the top of a white mountain skiing where the skies are bright blue, and the sun warms my heart and soul."

K

Korie Minkus

Just like with what you put into your body, this circle isn't about exercising to be skinny or "better." It's about being energized and alive to the world! And if you're exercising under those mindsets, raising your vibration level may even mean exercising *less*. Sitting in the sunshine, resting, being at peace with yourself and the world.

What do you need to let go of? What can you replace it with?

"I grew up in the Adirondacks, and I'll always have a soft spot for the mountains. As a young girl, I found peace and solace when connecting with nature. Now, I'm living the Florida salt life and enjoying it just as much. I practice Tai Chi to balance my physical energy within. Since I moved south, I draw energy and expansion from the external world in new ways. I spend time meditating by the water, because any type of flowing water feature, from the ocean to a small fountain, can help to connect with your physical body. By creating a beautiful space in the environment I inhabit, I create a positive reflection of myself, which helps to sort my outer world and calm my inner world."

L

Lisa Vrancken

Community means the way we connect to other people in the world, whether directly or indirectly. People can either expand or drain your energy. Natasha emphasized this idea in her interview with us for the WotB: Who are you hanging out with? You are an average of the five people you hang out with, so if they've all got great ambition, motivation, and positivity, you will raise your bar. If they're just drainers, complainers, or emitting toxic energy, your average is lowering every day. You choose your friends, so choose wisely. We all know what it's like to chat with someone who is living a low-vibration life and who is constantly negative. We leave the interaction feeling drained of our energy—and maybe it leaves *us* wanting to complain. On the other hand, we all know what it's like spending time with *expanders*—high-vibrational people who make you feel *good* about yourself. It can brighten your whole day. Take a look around you at all the "people" you consume. This is everything from the posts you consume on social media to the actors in the movies, the writers and subjects of the books you read, the text conversations you have, the work interactions you face daily. What aspect of your community do you need to adjust or give up? And what do you need to add?

"For me, the concept of community is a big and beautiful thing shared by many. At the same time, it can also be a very intimate and personal exchange. Community comes from a day spent at a conference with hundreds of people, all seeking to learn new ideas together, or even a simple conversation between people that easily flows and leaves them both glowing. I generate a lot of joy and high-vibrational energy from people in my life, both online and in person. I love interacting with women in WotB, where I've been fueled by a passion to truly hear their stories and dreams and share mine in return. Our community is our family, our friends, and our chosen connections with kindred souls. I've never been able to find a connection like the one I had with my mother, Rose. She was an incredible woman, confidant, and the jewel of my life. She's no longer with us on this earth, but she'd be proud to know the bond I share with my sister Frances is unbreakable. Through the ebbs and flows of life and business, Frances enriches my every day through a stronghold of love and authenticity. It provides great comfort knowing I always have someone in my corner with an open ear and honest words. My best friend Andrew always elevates my energy, too. We can talk and laugh for hours, about everything under the sun. He's absolutely my person."

"I believe one of the major reasons for the success of my business is the ten years leading up to my business. As a bodyworker, I was working with some of the most successful athletes of all time. Then actors, then billionaires and thought leaders in LA. When I was doing the body work, I got to intimately know clients; I would interview them about their journeys. They knew me well. They knew my ambitions. Being around these expansive people day in and day out was a game changer. I would say things like, 'I want to have my curriculum for fasciology become a licensed medical field.' Or 'I want to win the Nobel Prize.' My clients had already achieved so much in their own lives that their response was usually something like 'Yeah, I can totally see that' or 'Maybe I should introduce you to….' Being in the energy of people who have limitless beliefs allowed me to expand. My advice—get in the room with expanders! Virtual rooms count, books count! Inundate yourself with expanders!"

A

Ashley Black

"Investing in friendships and building community has always been an important part of my journey. Whether professional or personal, I live by Barbra Streisand's famous words: 'People who need people are the luckiest people in the world.' Professionally, I have found great mentors, from celebrities to less-known business millionaires and billionaires—all brilliant high achievers, willing to share wisdom and new ways of thinking. I am grateful for these friendships that afforded me an expanded toolbox that I get to pass on and share. And my personal friendships and community, as both a working mom and a woman seeking to stay relevant, have been a life source for me. I deeply honor and value these friendships, taking nothing for granted. Once, my girlfriends and I had a handwriting specialist who described our personality based on our writing. He called me the 'Garland Girl,' as my intuition has always led me to weave together perfect and beautifully unique groups of friends. Building community and relationships is always about patience, give-and-take, and acceptance. I am forever grateful for my tribe and the lessons I learn from investing in this fullness in my life. BTW, after thirty-three years staying in a committed marriage, I have learned the deepest sense of meaning behind redefining disappointment, that proximity does not equal presence, and that love can and should evolve."

K

Korie Minkus

It's like the age-old saying: "If you're the smartest person in the room, you need a new room." In this case, if you're the highest-vibrational person in the room, you need more high-vibrational people in your life—and you're going to have to go find new rooms to find them. We cannot stress enough that you need to add expanders into your life and cut off or block the energy of those who detract! It's not about good or bad people, it's about tuning forks: Which frequency do you want to match?

You might notice that each category somewhat overlaps with at least a few other categories. The reason for that is simple: everything is connected! The Five Circles of High-Vibrational Living are impossible to perfectly compartmentalize. Not only is our vibration affected by what our workspace looks like, it matters what we bring in for lunch, and it matters who we are eating lunch with. No circle can exist without the other circles, and no life is in harmony without all energies vibrating at high levels. Let us repeat: ALL energies vibrating at high levels.

Keep in mind that nothing here is prescriptive. We know, thanks not only to science but to our own experiences, that certain energies make us *feel good.* The purpose of the chart (and of this book) is not to offer cut-and-dry instructions on how to live the perfect life, or to offer judgment if you do anything "wrong." The goal is to help you to become aware of how you're living your life and ask yourself whether it's in line with the highest version of self. "Should" is the language of shame, which is one of the lowest-vibrational emotions. So rather than think, "I should be exercising more," ask yourself,

"How do I *feel* when I move my body this way?" Rather than think, "I should eat more vegetables," ask yourself, "How do I *feel* when I eat certain foods?" We invite you, without judgments or attachments, to scan all the areas of your life like a detective and see where you can make conscious adjustments. Far too often women feel trapped or stuck in their business or their life, when the one actually causing the roadblock...is themselves. How can you raise your vibration level to maximize your success? If you are living a high-vibrational life across the board, you can't help but be successful as an entrepreneur. Don't get us wrong, raising your vibration is not easy, but it's much easier to manifest the things you desire most when you can attract them like a tuning fork.

In order to solidify your commitment to living a high-vibrational life, we've devised a Movement for this chapter that will ask you to reflect on the energies you're engaging with throughout your day and how they can be raised, so that you can be in a space to receive, attract, and expand. Come on ladies, we're moving up. Let's work on our plan for ascending to a high-vibrational life.

MOVEMENT #2: VIBRATION TRACKER

In chapter one, we discussed the importance of tracking your brain waves throughout the day. This Movement serves as a continuation of that exercise; just as it's important to understand how much of your day is spent in brainless beta mode, being aware of the vibration you're operating at throughout your day will help you to live a more fulfilled life.

"Balance or something close to it takes many years of practice. It won't happen overnight, but it's about getting on a path that feels fulfilling for your mind, body, and spirit. Incorporating mindful practices, one by one, and building on your knowledge are the best ways to achieve it. Through biohacking, we harness the power to truly self-regulate. I've learned firsthand how hacking your mind will help you to channel certain states, inviting you to tap into greater peace and productivity. I believe technology can be a gift and a curse, and it's necessary to use vibrational awareness to see what works and what doesn't. In my free time, I go all-in to understand and embrace tech that improves our lives. My client, Brain Health Sciences, gifted me a headset that uses a neuro-algorithm scientifically proven to help achieve perfectly balanced brain wave states. I absolutely love the vibe, and it's a great way to disconnect when you're feeling low from too much scrolling and screen time."

L

Lisa Vrancken

In the chart below, you'll see sections dedicated to the Five Circles of High-Vibrational Living. For this exercise, we will ask you to describe how the five influences factor into your day; the goal, again, is to bring more AWARENESS and mindfulness to your life. This is NOT for you to critique and judge yourself. Feel free to flow and write the first thing that pops into your mind, *before* you start to dissect it (we women do that sometimes). Here's your chance to craft your "Raise My Vibration Plan" and set in motion some intentional elevations.

Just like with Movement #1, this is not a one-and-done Movement. This is a chart you can do over and over as you evolve, as a "check" to ensure that your vibrational frequency matches the life you want to create—a life of passion and purpose and products and prosperity. Real ascension is not only slow, but constant, and taking stock of your vibrational levels is an activity we encourage you to do regularly in order to stay balanced and whole as you embark on starting or scaling your business. Becoming high-vibrational in all the areas of your life will create MORE energy and give your elevation momentum. Having a high vibration and momentum will allow you to flow as you embark on the difficulties in the "real world" of business, and will solidify and expand your passions.

Movement #2 Vibration Tracker

Five Circles of High-Vibrational Living	Describe the place, thing, feeling, person, etc.	Is my vibration level high, medium, or low around this influence?	Describe the effect this influence has on my vibration.	Is this an area where I need to raise my vibration level?
Environment (not just the physical places, but the energies of those places as well)				
General environment		**High** **Medium** **Low**		**Yes** **No**
Workplace/creative space		**High** **Medium** **Low**		**Yes** **No**
In solitude		**High** **Medium** **Low**		**Yes** **No**

For your consideration

FOR YOUR CONSIDERATION: Take a few moments to reflect on the work you just did for this Movement. Look at the words you just wrote. What three words that you have added to the chart above ignite your passion the most? Write them here:		
1.	2.	3.

❁ CHAPTER THREE ❁

BE...Passionate

Lara Eurdolian

Lara Eurdolian is a beauty expert, blogger, and founder of the massively successful Pretty Connected. But success didn't happen instantaneously; it was a process of learning new things and following her curiosity wherever it led...and where it led was something she could be passionate about—and something, it turned out, that other people could get passionate about, too! "I started my beauty blog in 2007 as a way to share with my friends and fellow beauty junkies everything I was learning about new products from being embedded in the industry. I didn't know at the time that Pretty Connected would become a brand, or that it would lead to the launch of my own line of accessories." After achieving recognition for Pretty Connected, Lara kept chasing her passion for fashion, and by staying curious and trying new things, she was able to make even bigger waves in the fashion industry: "At the time, I was taking my Sony A600 camera to all these fashion events," Lara recalls. "It had this gaudy, overtly branded strap. I wanted something simple and chic that I could change depending on my outfit, but there was nothing like that available on the market. So, I started making my own camera straps out of thin but sturdy chains, and I'd attach little charms for that extra flare. Everywhere I went, people always wanted

to know where they could buy my camera chains. After a couple of years, I finally decided to take the plunge. I began looking into how I could put them into production." By following her curiosity without forcing any answers, Lara was able to develop her passion into a purposeful product that everyone around her loved. "My philosophy has always been to nurture every seed, because you never know what amazing opportunities will bloom," Lara says. Cultivating a business that is rooted in passion is a process—one that can't be forced, but followed with trust in the universe and in yourself. Stick with us as we talk more in this chapter about how to transform curiosity into a thriving passion!

instagram.com/prettyconnected
instagram.com/prettyconnectedshop

PRACTICING PASSION

We've spent a lot of time talking about the role of Divine Feminine energy, brain waves, and high-vibrational living in discovering your passion. But...what does it actually *mean* to be passionate? Let's dig it out together.

It may seem like a simple question, but Merriam-Webster's definition of passion as "a strong liking or desire" hardly seems to contain all the power of passionate living. And when we ask the women in WotB what their passions are, we get some vague answers. Many women will say, "I am passionate about helping others," or "I am passionate about living well," or even just, "I want to be happy." But what do these things actually entail? What does it mean, "to be happy?" The answers we got from the women in WotB led us to believe that we needed to help you ladies transition from something elusive to something you can identify and manifest more of.

> *"Over the years I have been exposed to and engaged in silent retreats and devoted time for personal development work. But where I get into my truest cognitive state and become clear in problem-solving is when I am in moments of quiet contemplation while walking the golf course with my beloved sons. They both learned golf at the age of two, and since then, I have been totally dedicated to my presence with them in the place they are happiest. Happy Kids = Happy Mom. This place helps me be clear in memory, break down complex situations, and fuel my 'why' to drive clarity for my passion. This time and place is sacred to me. What's yours?"*
>
> **K**
>
> **Korie Minkus**

It's different for everyone. One woman's passion might be another's half-hearted chore. Like cooking, for instance. Some women, like Lisa, might get into an alpha meditation and creative flow while they cook, and other women dread cooking. For some women, engaging with a work project might channel high, beta brain waves; these women are challenged and passionate about the process, like Korie, whereas others might be watching the clock and dreaming of just kicking back. Some women, like Ashley, might enjoy a day of riding the back roads of Costa Rica and surfing, riding that alpha/theta wave, and some women might find that terrifying, hot, and miserable. So, if everyone's passions are different, and everyone experiences high vibrations through different activities, where do we start?

Well, the only mistake is to not start at all. As the old adage goes, "Insanity is doing the same thing over and over and expecting different results." This insanity is the same insanity involved in Time to Make the Donuts mode: When you carry out the same routine over and over and over again, with the same thinking over and over and over again, you're traveling the same neurological pathways and achieving the same outcomes each time. It's a form of self-torture to not live your most authentic life and to not reach your highest potential, and that potential is probably A LOT higher than you think. But the idea of growing can be scary—even downright terrifying for some of us. Our low-vibrational Little Bitchy Voice chimes in: *What if I try something new and hate it? What if I waste my time? I don't like things like that. I don't have to try that right now.* And our favorite, *That's not going to pay the mortgage.*

We are here to tell you that trying new things is not just important. It's crucial. Getting into your gamma, your alpha, and your theta will help you achieve the vibrations necessary to attract the life you really want. If you're in Time to Make the Donuts mode, you're going to attract Time to Make the Donuts energy. This isn't woo-woo, it's physics.

"Research shows theta waves are active when we remember emotional experiences. Theta is involved with creativity, healing, and creating 'cognitive maps' that are important for memory as a form of architecture. When I'm cultivating this brain wave, I write poetry and voraciously read to enter a dreamy, trancelike theta flow state where I can untangle any difficult emotions and find my way back to my passion.

I get my alpha energy flowing by biking and going horseback riding. My three-year-old great-niece Everly Rose is the joy of my life; spending time with her is an infinite infusion of pure, innocent, magical alpha energy. Engaging in play with younger family members is a great way to access alpha. When I step into Everly's world of imagination, anything and everything becomes possible. And when I'm working to generate power in the crown chakra, I light sandalwood incense and practice daily meditation to access my highest state of consciousness—full-on, focused gamma insight. Ahhh, what a high!"

L

Lisa Vrancken

"One of the most incredible things I've learned and put into practice is creating new neural pathways. I love anything science-based, and as the scientific community evolves there is just more and more validation that doing new things creates a new neural network, which creates growth. At the beginning of each week, as a plan, I intentionally do three new things. It could be as simple as scheduling a podcast that explores a topic I would like to learn more about, or it could be more dramatic like hiking a waterfall I've never been to. But the key for me is that it's intentional. If you intentionally do three new things a week in business and in life, you will be shocked to see how your life cracks open and exponentially expands! But it's a weekly practice—a discipline."

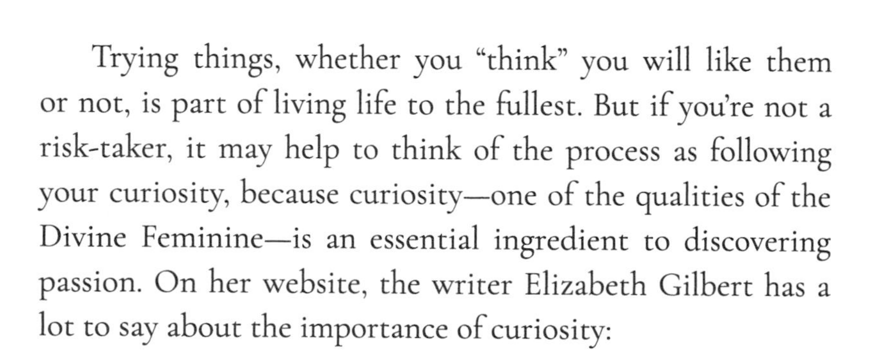

Ashley Black

Trying things, whether you "think" you will like them or not, is part of living life to the fullest. But if you're not a risk-taker, it may help to think of the process as following your curiosity, because curiosity—one of the qualities of the Divine Feminine—is an essential ingredient to discovering passion. On her website, the writer Elizabeth Gilbert has a lot to say about the importance of curiosity:

> In seasons of confusion, of loss, of boredom, of insecurity, of distraction, the idea of 'passion' can feel completely inaccessible and impossible.... But curiosity, I have found, is always within reach. Passion is a tower of flame, but curiosity is a tiny tap on the shoulder—a little whisper in the ear that says, 'Hey, that's kind of interesting....' Passion is rare; curiosity is everyday. Curiosity is therefore a lot easier to reach at times than full-on passion—and the stakes are lower, easier to manage.

We love the way she frames this. So, LET'S GET CURIOUS. What makes your brain whir with excitement and interest? What do you want to learn more about? What is that thing that you shied away from because you thought someone would judge you? What was that thing that you used to love to do but don't anymore? It's time to be curious like a child, looking for wonder in every moment. This is the natural state of a human being, so let's connect with our curiosity as a first step.

In the previous two chapters, we've taken stock of our lives and discovered where our time and energy are currently going. You might have realized you're spending a lot more time in beta mode than you originally thought, or that you're slogging through low vibrations for most of the day, or that you need to surround yourself with more expanders. How do you manifest the life you want to live?

"The personal development journey for me was about learning to accept and love what I did not like about myself so that I could clear the way for what could be. Through this process, I discovered how much time I invested in the parts of me I did not approve of—that little bitchy voice that was always judging. Why did it take me over forty years to release all the judgment and realize how liberating this can BE? I thought back to when I was a figure skater. Learning to do a double axel requires an extreme level of precision, coordination, and self-trust. Who knew one could thrust themselves off a single blade, fly into the air, and visualize landing back on one blade? And believe me, what did I learn from that experience? After falling on the cold and hard ice, bruising both my body and ego, I learned that if you wanted to succeed, there was only one choice. Get up and do it again. I was extremely passionate about skating. It was literally my first love. It was not about someone else; it was for me, by me. Through from my passion for this sport and my highly competitive nature, skating taught me a mental confidence and a deep sense of self-respect. Find that deep sense that drives you to this place and experience this brilliance of ascension. It's magical. Nothing can stop you!"

K

Six words: *BE it until you become it.*

This may seem like contradictory advice coming from a book so hell-bent on living authentically, but when you think about it, it's the only way we grow. When people talk about "passion," they often don't realize it isn't some magical thing that just *happens*, but that it's a practice you must develop like any other. It's something you learn. Just like anything new, you might not know what your passion is until, well, you play the role for a while. By "play the role" we don't mean living inauthentically. We mean creating new possibilities, trusting yourself, and trusting the process—engaging your balanced brain waves often, and choosing to live as high-vibrational and expansive a life as you can. Oprah Winfrey said, "Passion is energy. Feel the power that comes from focusing on what excites you." When you follow your balanced brain waves and live high-vibrationally in alignment with your Divine Feminine energy, your passion will reveal itself to you. The more you expand, the more you receive the thing you want, so before we focus on what you want, let's focus on the EXPANSION itself.

MOVEMENT #3: 2 + 2

Discovering passion isn't an exact science, and there's *loads* more we haven't even talked about in this chapter, including heart alignment and collective consciousness. But when you combine the curiosity and creativity of alpha brain waves with high-vibrational living, exploring your passion is rather simple—as simple as two plus two. Let's break that down: when you balance your **brain waves** and expand your daily consumption of "new" things, and then put that expansive mindset into **action** to achieve a higher vibration, the result will be **PASSION**, baby. Passion WILL reveal itself. But it's up to you to commit to the process of digging it out.

Brain Waves + High-Vibration Action = Passion

This Movement represents the final push toward pinpointing your passion. As a reminder, none of the brain waves we discussed in chapter one are "bad" or "wrong." We need them all at different moments throughout the day—even low beta. But alpha and theta are integral to playing, creating, and developing passion as well as establishing new beliefs. In this Movement, we have broken down three qualities of alpha/theta mode that are central to cultivating passion: **playfulness**, **creativity**, and **fantasy**. We invite you to identify moments throughout your day or life where you are most playful, are most creative, and daydream the most—or maybe you're not doing *any* of those things, in which case we have our work cut out for us, don't we. Thinking about the Five Circles of High-Vibrational Living; what are the scenarios that allow you to enter these childlike mindsets? For instance, maybe you notice that you don't feel very playful when you're scrolling social media, because it causes you to zone out or to judge yourself too much. Maybe you feel more playful when you spend time with your husband, who encourages you to be silly and have fun and take risks. Maybe you feel more creative after midnight than at eight in the morning, or you daydream more when you watch less television. Maybe you're trapped in beta mode the majority of the day and feel you don't have the time or energy to engage in play.

"Getting a good amount of sleep will give your brain a healthy dose of delta waves, which can help us access our spiritual minds. I think it's so cool there are more delta waves in the brains of meditators and intuitive healers than on average. It's why I practice dream journaling—to remember my subconscious revelations while swimming in the deep deltas of my mind.

I brainstorm in beta, taking lots of calls and consulting with clients who are facing different daily challenges. But after a long day of beta attention and focus, I love letting it all go in an alpha kickboxing flow. It's a great way to have a natural brain chemical release of serotonin and endorphins."

Lisa Vrancken

There's an infinite number of ways you could fill out this chart (and nobody will fill out the chart the same way you do!). Just like the other Movements, this is one you'll probably want to repeat multiple times as you continue to manifest your dream future.

Movement #3 2+2

Think about your everyday schedule: How much energy do you waste in Time to Make the Donuts mode? As we've said, beta mode is often unavoidable, and even good! But too much time there will leave you feeling like a zombie. So how can you trim off some of that beta fat? Identify three activities you perform in beta mode that you can cut from your schedule.
1. 2. 3.
Ahh! We've shaved off some of that beta slag and now we feel free as a bird. Think about all the fun new activities you can do in the time you've reclaimed! Now that you've cut those beta activities, what are three things you can add to your day to engage your playful Alpha or dreamy Theta?
1. 2. 3.

> *"The first time I did the 'trim the beta fat' movement, it was years ago and it was dramatic. I gave up traffic, alarm clocks, and driving. You may say, 'How the hell do you do that?' But with intentionality you can do anything. It was one of the best things I ever did, and 90 percent of the time I still do it. Sitting in traffic was the biggest waste of time, and I just made my schedule more flexible so I didn't have to travel in high-traffic times, even scheduling meetings and flights around rush hour. I hated being jolted out of REM sleep right into activity, so I decided to shift my schedule to allow for more free and ME time in the morning. And giving up driving was incredible. I sold my cars and hired a driver or took Ubers. Now, many years later, I still wake up to the sun, I don't drive except my ATV down the dirt roads of Costa Rica, and the only traffic I encounter is cows. Unbelievable the amount of energy I reclaimed! And I trim the beta fat more and more every year."*

Ashley Black

You'll get tired of us saying this, but it's true: this Movement isn't a one-time exercise, but an exercise you should keep doing periodically as you follow your path to prosperity. The tricky thing about Time to Make the Donuts mode and Zombie mode is that they often begin as activities we perform with alertness, or even joy, but it's scary-easy for activities we do often to become rote and mechanical or for us to feel burned out on activities we love if we don't get any rest from them. In the next chapter, we're going to talk about how to keep finding purpose and meaning in the day-to-day, even when it feels like you're just going through the motions of life. But we encourage you to come back to this chart again as you keep chasing your bliss.

For your consideration

FOR YOUR CONSIDERATION: Take a few moments to reflect on the work you just did for this Movement. Look at the words you just wrote. What three words that you have added to the chart above ignite your passion the most? Write them here:		
1.	2.	3.

PART II

Purpose

❀ CHAPTER FOUR ❀

BE...Intentional

Vera Moore

Hey there! Welcome to Part II: Purpose. To kick off chapter four, we've sat down with Vera Moore, the founder of Vera Moore Cosmetics—a cosmetics line specifically targeted to women of color—and a huge testament to the power of applying intentionality to passion! While Vera paved the way for modern brands like Black Opal and IMAN, she didn't always plan to be an entrepreneur: "The idea of creating a cosmetics and skincare line for women of color only came to me after I had landed the role of Nurse Linda Metcalf on NBC's *Another World*. This was the early 1970s, and for a black woman to be cast in a lead role on a daytime soap opera was groundbreaking." Moore was already making history in her acting career, but she noticed another arena where she could make a meaningful difference: "When I sat down in the makeup chair, there was only one option available to me. One choice is no choice. I realized there was a gap in the beauty market, and the need to fill it kept pulling on the strings of my heart." We love how Vera translated her daily experiences and observations into an authentic personal brand (more on personal branding in chapter seven) that led to a thriving, world-changing business venture! In the next three chapters, we're going to really dive into what it means to live a purposeful life—and how you, too, can parlay your passion and purpose into your product.

instagram.com/veramoorecos
facebook.com/VeraMooreCosmetics

YOU'VE FOUND YOUR PASSION—NOW WHAT?

Just like with passion, lots of people, when asked to define what their "purpose" is, give some pretty vague answers. So before we dive into discovering our purpose, we ought to explain what exactly we mean by "purpose" in the first place.

One way to think of purpose is as *passion with intentionality*: if passion is living high-vibrationally, purpose is how you *assign meaning* to the passion. Passion is something you feel—your inner light radiating—and purpose, meanwhile, is the application of that light to the contribution of the things you care about. For a simple example, your passion might be helping others. So when you perform acts like a guiding conversation, you attribute that time spent to your purpose. You could say, then, that one of your purposes is making the world a better place. OR another example is that if you feel passionate about decorating, then you will feel purposeful when you enrich the life of your client by creating a beautiful space. OR you could be more specific, like Ashley, who is passionate about educating her customers about the fascia system, and whose purpose is to improve the health care system. It's all about taking the things that excite us and framing them as part of the greater good—our purpose. Or purpose*s*!

> *"Purposefully living for me was becoming aware of how much of the time my mind wandered to some other place while I was otherwise engaged with people or activities. My mind would race to all those things that I had to do or all the things I thought I needed to be thinking about. I began to experience how wonderful it felt when I was totally present to appreciate even the simplest moments in life. This became more obvious for me when I did my first two-week cleanse in my thirties. It was vivid as day, after the cleanse, the incredible explosive sensation I experienced with each bite of flavor. Each bite reminded me of the appreciation for the experience eating offers. This sense of presence gave me an elevated relationship to living purposefully, even in each daily routine or activity. Simplicity and presence can be a hidden treasure and slice of heaven."*
>
> **K**
>
> **Korie Minkus**

Now we're not generally ones to nitpick, but we've got to clear something up: there's a difference between *having a purpose* and *living purposefully*, but we all need to do both. Having a purpose is the "Grand Plan," where purposeful living is moment-by-moment. While having a purpose refers more to living out your passion to contribute to the world in some way, purposeful living refers to applying meaning to your everyday routine. The Grand Plan will reveal itself, if it already hasn't, but we want to take a moment to focus on purposeful living. That includes actions that you take for granted (like eating dinner with your family), or even activities that you dislike (like commuting to and from work). It's easy to sail through family dinners in beta mode. And it's easy to become Zombified when you're stuck in a traffic jam. We can even zone out to things that should bring us joy, like a good conversation, if we're too distracted in our brain. So how do you make these simple—or even downright unpleasant—activities meaningful?

Meaning isn't always given—it's something we construct ourselves through our perspective. Meaning-making *is* inherently a Divine Feminine act, so if you want to live purposefully, it's time to shake off your masculine energy and channel your feminine side. Think back to the masculine-feminine energies chart from page **27**. When our masculine and feminine energies are out of alignment, we experience that inner conflict: Being too masculine can keep us in a constant state of productivity and logic, and meaning-making requires the mindfulness and grace of the Divine Feminine (as they say, "You're a human being, not a human doing.") So if you're channeling your masculine energy all day, put it on pause and shift into Divine Feminine mode. A full and purposeful life demands that you produce *and* receive, think *and* feel, do *and* BE. Being an expander is all about daily advancements in our actions and accepting and receiving the meaning that comes from those actions. And then what do expanders do? Expand more! New actions, new meaning, new purpose. Strap in, ladies!

> *"We really do create our own reality, and our reality is a reflection of our perception. Plain and simple—I assign meaning to everything I do, or I don't do it. If I'm making a meal for Jordi, I view it as a privilege to serve him and spoil him. If I'm doing a grinding task with my business, I view it as a stepping-stone to a greater good. If I'm taking a break in my day and napping, it's for the purpose of nourishing my body. The way you approach life is 100 percent your decision."*
>
> A
>
> **Ashley Black**

Maybe you used to find meaning in your job, but lately... you're just not feeling it. Maybe your relationship has lost its spark—all you and your partner ever talk about anymore is bills and whose turn it is to load the dishwasher, and you don't feel connected on an emotional level. Maybe you've been distracted by the demands of work and home life and have let your friendships fall by the wayside. Do you give up? Cut your losses and start over?

"As a working mom, one question I often get is, 'How do you do it all?' Well, certainly not gracefully at times. Especially when talking about turning on and off or leaning into both the Divine Feminine and Masculine. Where I struggled the most was transitioning from the imprisonment from my masculine self all day in the corporate setting, to light my spark of Divine Feminine at home. I masked this difficulty by investing in personal development and physical fitness; however, I really supercharged this alignment when I left corporate and became an entrepreneur. I discovered a new sense of purposefulness that allowed me to be more grounded in my authentic self—gaining alignment and achieving balance that had disappeared. This shift was so massive for me. In March of 2018, six months after I took on this new life, I was traveling in Israel, speaking at an event in Tel Aviv, when I woke the second day of the event to the room spinning. I got full-blown Vertigo that was triggered from the emotional shifts and increased adrenaline levels caused by this life-altering experience." (cont.)

Korie Minkus

"My body reacted with a fight-or-flight response to wanting to hold on to the old ways and trying to find footing in the new ones. It was frightening and forever life-changing, recognizing how far off my axis point I had allowed my life to become. This shift to a more balanced existence remodeled my life and, from that moment on, my commitment to self has been with deep appreciation of living purposefully aligned and of honoring my intuitive actions of feminine and masculine harmony."

K

Korie Minkus

Sure, sometimes an inability to find meaning is an indication that it's time to move on to a new chapter of life. But other times, when we can't see the purpose in an activity or relationship or career anymore, it just means we need to reframe the situation and learn how to breathe new life into it. You can take new action in your current situations as well as add new situations. If you're feeling dull at a job you once loved, what improvements could you make to give it more purpose? Propose a project to your boss or, if you're an entrepreneur, make a pivot and try a new audience or new networking group. Maybe your romantic relationship has begun to feel dull: It could be time to try something new together. Try a cooking class, a staycation, go dancing—anything to break the routine. Maybe you used to love going to the gym and now it's a grind; try a new activity, like aerial yoga or wall climbing, or start working out with a buddy or a group, or take a class. We don't know your personal situation, but remember, YOU have to be the vibration you want to attract. If you want to see real growth, you can't keep bringing the same low vibration to your situation. BUT if you bring a higher vibration to the situation, you can expect a shift one way or the other; like the tuning fork, either the vibration level of the person or environment you engage with will rise to match your high frequency or the person or environment will be repulsed. That second outcome is never fun, but in the end, the only person you're in charge of is yourself. So if you're stuck in the same old drudgery or low-vibrational living, don't just accept it! Raise your vibration levels, ladies, and let the chips fall where they fall.

"Whether you're talking about walking the path that unveils our Grand Plan or living purposefully in everyday moments, it all starts with intention. Sometimes it may seem like you've been intentional as the architect of your beautiful life, and yet you wake up feeling like you've been doing it wrong all along. Meaning is derived as you go, and sometimes it requires a good pivot.

There's no reason to be afraid of the change that awaits you. After four years of undergrad and three years working towards a law degree in my twenties, I had a big realization: I no longer wanted to be a civil rights lawyer. I had become intimately aware of the inequalities in the judicial system, especially for low-income women. I thought I was following my passion, but when I nearly completed the journey, I had to pivot. I listened to the call of my Divine Feminine intuition and started making my way in a different direction.

You may spend years trying to get through a certain door, only to realize that it's not the right room for you. As we grow, our purpose evolves. The destination may look different during each chapter of your life; we can have multiple passions that allow us to live our purpose in different ways. When you find what resonates, allow it to ignite the torch of promise. That's the light you follow."

Lisa Vrancken

> *"Although it's easy to blame your situation on others or external factors, when you take full accountability for your life, you realize what happens to you is because you caused it. Hard pill to swallow. My last five years in corporate, I resented a lot, felt abused and out of alignment. I questioned my purpose often. This should have been a big* WARNING SIGN *for me, but as I made the donuts, I didn't realize what was happening. Lesson I learned—when this is happening, step up your self-accountability, as you have a choice. Exercise it. Or regrets can follow. During this five-year period, I almost destroyed my health, marriage, and blew up my family, all seeking to find fulfillment and control, when all along, it was right in front of me. Trust your instinct."*
>
> **K**
>
> **Korie Minkus**

This might sound drastic, but it doesn't have to be. *Your life doesn't necessarily need a major overhaul to develop new meaning.* Living purposefully doesn't just mean approaching your everyday schedule more mindfully; it might also involve cutting (or at least cutting back on) activities that you don't find fulfilling, or only find fulfilling in smaller doses. For instance, a little television might be a great way to unwind. Or maybe you watch with your friends or family, so it's a good opportunity to socialize and cultivate intimacy. But check in with yourself after two or three or five episodes of *Real Housewives* (or a whole season...yeah, we've been there): Are you still able to find meaning in this activity? Does it have a purpose? Or would you feel more fulfilled ceasing and engaging in something else? This might seem like a silly example, but you have to keep in mind that you only have a certain amount of time and energy in the day, so to live purposefully, you have to transfer lower-vibrational activities to higher ones, little by little. Reclaiming your time is a CHOICE you must make to ascend and expand!

We've given you loads of examples, ranging from the extreme to the mundane. But there's no direct line to meaningful living—we can't say, "Cut out *Real Housewives* or you'll never be high-vibrational." If only it were that easy, right? The only rock-solid way to start living a purposeful life is to become *aware*—aware of your brain waves throughout the day, and aware of the vibrations you're soaking up and emitting.

Remember how we talked about neuroplasticity in chapter one? Well, living your life more intentionally may require some neural rewiring, but it *is* possible! Making standard or unpleasant tasks meaningful can imbue your day (and life!) with a sense of purpose, fulfillment, and grace.

So let's dive in!

"As a nurturing soul, it took a while for me to realize I had been giving away so much of my life source energy to others in a way that left me drained. And yet, I love helping people, it's in my DNA...which may seem like a contradiction! My takeaway is that you can only truly feel your purpose flowing through when you make time to hear yourself. You can only uplift others when you yourself are rising. And when it comes to big change, I advise taking a quantum leap only when you intuitively know it's right. Until then, make small and sustainable changes. Direct your creative flame into you. Make healthier choices about how to give your energy, so you can build from within. You can only unlock passion and purpose with a nourished mind, body, and spirit, and don't rush it! It may take some rearranging to get there."

MOVEMENT #4: MEANING-MAKER

It's a sad fact of life that being a modern human involves a *lot* of mundanity. Most of us have experienced the fatigue or numbness of doing the same thankless tasks over and over again, or performing the same ritualistic activities to the point they lose their significance. So how do we pull ourselves out of Time to Make the Donuts mode and find meaning in the mundane? How do we stop treating family dinners, our daily commute, and reading to the children before bedtime as simple chores or dull everyday activities that can be taken for granted, and instead regard them with gratitude and wonder? It might seem strange to talk about meaning as something you make rather than as an inherent quality, but the truth is that gratitude and wonder are learned abilities. In this Movement, we will practice finding meaning in the mundane by engaging with our daily tasks more purposefully.

By this point in the book, you know we're a big fan of "awareness charts." This time, we've created a chart that will help you analyze your daily schedule so you can begin to create more purpose, regardless of what stage you're at in your life or business. We've given you sixteen time slots to account for sixteen waking hours, assuming you're getting eight solid hours of sleep at night (and hopefully you are). To help you get started, we've started filling out our own chart, below:

Movement #4 Meaning-Maker

Daily schedule	Why do I do these activities?	What brain wave(s) associate with these activities?	Is this an activity that contributes to my passions? What purpose does this contribute to?	What feeling(s) is/are elicited by this activity? Are these high-vibrational feelings, or do I need to re-examine?	Does this activity contribute to my purpose(s) in life? Do I need to reframe or delete it from my life?
Time: 6:00 a.m. Wake up—- meditate	To set my day in motion in a good headspace	Gamma, alpha	Yes— - meditation is crucial for me to express gratitude and receive inner wisdom.	Calm, peace, self-control This is definitely something I want/need in my day.	Purposeful.
7:00 a.m. Breakfast with family	Basic need and to be close to family	Beta, alpha	Yes— - I am passionate about caring for my family. And this contributes to my purpose of contributing to society through my children.	Right now, I need to address the stress in this activity and shift to gratitude. I need to apply purpose to this task and live in the present while I do this	I need to reframe this activity. This activity could bring great joy to me. I am going to bring a higher vibration to this activity.
8:00 a.m. Scroll social media	To feel relevant on social events and know what my friends are up to.	Beta	No— - just makes me compare myself to others and waste time.	Anxiety, jealousy, resentment, frustration, shame	Not purposeful. Need to limit this activity and reframe it to look at higher-vibrational content.

Our day started at 6:00 a.m. and ended at 10:00 p.m. and included activities like "driving to work" and "scrolling social media." Your day might start earlier or later and many of your tasks will differ. Once you've filled out your daily schedule, apply the following questions to each activity to determine if the activity serves you or not: Is it a task that imbues your life with purpose? If not, can you apply meaning to it, or can you cut it?

Meaning-Maker Blank

Daily schedule	Why do I do these activities?	What brain wave(s) do I associate with these activities?	Is this an activity that serves me?	What is the greater meaning behind it?	Does it raise my vibration level? Is this activity purposeful/intentional?
Time:					
Time:					
Time:					
Time:					
Time:					
Time:					
Time:					

You won't be able to control everything in your life. You may not be able to magically transform the fact that you have to drive to work every day, or pay bills, or caretake a sick parent, or pick up after the dog. But you can shift your perspective and therefore the feelings you have surrounding everything you do. It's all about bringing total mindfulness to all of your activities, whether work-related, entrepreneur-related, or for charity, family, friends—ALL of it. Shifting your perspective about the things you need to do to keep the balls rolling, completely cutting the things that lower your vibration, and introducing new things every day WILL lead you to a purposeful life. We know we've thrown a lot of charts and Movements at you, but there is no easy recipe for discovering your purpose and living a more expansive life. But there is a path, and this is it. YOU and only YOU can dictate how and where you focus your energy and how you assign meaning to that energy. Take a moment and breathe that in.

For your consideration

FOR YOUR CONSIDERATION: Take a few moments to reflect on the work you just did for this Movement. Look at the words you just wrote. What three words that you have added to the chart above ignite your passion the most? Write them here:		
1.	2.	3.

❀ CHAPTER FIVE ❀

BE...Unlimited

Michelle Masters

Personal Development Coach and Bestselling Author

Michelle Masters is an internationally bestselling author, personal development trainer, and life coach specializing in neuroscience-based technologies. She is also a dear friend and mentor. We've featured her in the WotB and are in absolute AWE of the work she's done with neuro-linguistic programming (NLP), a process of identifying the subconscious biases and revising the self-limiting beliefs imprinted during early childhood. She specializes in growth and fixed mindsets, and overcoming limiting beliefs—which we'll explore more of in this chapter. "If we don't have a strong sense of worth, we will continually question if we're deserving," Michelle says. "When we question our worth, we project that negative perception onto others. In turn, they too question our worth, and by extension, the value of our products. The limiting beliefs you have about yourself will show up in your product pricing, the customers you attract, and even your employees.... Once you revise your patterning, the struggles in decision-making start to align and the universe conspires to help you. It's like having the wind at your back pushing you forward. You'll project a much more authentic version of who you are, and you'll realize we're all infinitely worthy." Just like

Michelle, we believe overcoming limiting beliefs is the first step to living your most authentic and purposeful life. In this chapter, we'll do a deep dive into what exactly limiting beliefs are, how to identify them, and how to stop them in their tracks.

facebook.com/michellemastersnlp

LIMITING BELIEFS

I don't have time.
That idea will fail.
The universe is working against me.
I don't know anything about that topic.

If you're like many people, these are some of the limiting beliefs you may have from time to time—maybe more often than you'd care to admit. Some may not even realize they think this way, because usually limiting beliefs are in the subconscious. Most people don't choose in the conscious brain to be self-limiting. We don't wake up and say, "How can I sabotage myself today?"

Limiting beliefs is not a new idea; in fact, it goes way back to Egyptian culture, and the Sumerian texts. Ancient Indian philosophy and Buddhism describe **samskaras** (Sanskrit: संस्कार) as mental impressions, recollections, psychological imprints, or formations. In Pali, there is a similar belief that is referred to as Saṅkhāra. These cultures all describe mental patterns as the groove of a record player scarred into our subconscious and played out over and over. Even the ancient philosophers knew that it was difficult to overcome these samskaras and that they could affect our behavior for a lifetime. These ancient ideas have even more weight today as society has become so much more complex. So how do we move the needle out of these grooves and make new grooves, creating the life we want? How do we create freedom from our samskaras?

Surprise, it's neuroplasticity to the rescue once again. It's possible through awareness and discipline to overcome our limiting beliefs about the world and about ourselves. So, you might be wondering, why don't more people do it? It may sound crazy, but limiting beliefs can actually feel cozy. A lot of people don't want to do the work to reforge their samskaras because that work can be challenging, and they would prefer to stay in their comfort zone. We know what you might be thinking: *What? How is telling myself I'm not enough comforting?* And you're right. It's not. But oftentimes, our motivation for limiting self-talk is to keep ourselves from taking risks and being vulnerable. We become *comfortable* in our limiting beliefs. Without our limiting beliefs we are free to be limitless, and being limitless can be...well, a little daunting. However, the thing is, you can't discover your passions and you can't fulfill your purpose if you're bogged down by limiting beliefs about who you truly are and what you're truly capable of. You can choose to bring these limiting beliefs to light and you can choose to overcome them. So in this chapter, we are going to help you unearth those limiting beliefs out of your subconscious, neutralize them, and replace them with new beliefs.

When we talk about limiting beliefs or samskaras, we're not talking about the belief that a stove is too hot to touch or that jumping off a cliff is dangerous. We're talking about the beliefs you have about yourself that might keep you unable to move forward in life and achieve the ultimate success and happiness you are capable of creating—you know, that Little Bitchy Voice. We develop most of our limiting beliefs in childhood up to about age eight—which, as you may remember from chapter one, is the same age by which our delta, theta, and alpha brain waves develop. These are the brain waves in which we are most receptive to new ideas and belief patterns.

In order to overcome our limiting beliefs as adults, we need to examine what we may have downloaded in those formative years. When children play "dragon" in their theta waves, that dragon is 100 percent real to them. When they discover something in their curious alpha waves, they download that, too, as absolute truth—for instance, that bees are scary or playing in the rain is messy. And so the samskaras form. Those examples might not seem too severe, but imagine if the messages you internalized in alpha and theta were more detrimental, like that abuse and suffering are acceptable, or that never having enough is conventional, or that you don't deserve good things. We play out our lives according to these grooves we developed in childhood, and the things we attract align with those grooves. So as we start the labor of rewiring our brains for the better, let's take a little journey through our beliefs, and begin to lift that needle out of the groove.

"I was raised in the North Shore—an idyllic area of Chicago. A middle child with two brothers I adored, I lived in a loving, tight-knit household. My family had achieved the American dream. My father was a CFO for multinational corporations and my mother a dedicated wife and mom. By virtue of my family's success, I was expected to do great things. At the age of four, I started figure skating and fell in love with the femininity and grace of the sport. I quickly became addicted to skating and the discipline and dedication to excel. Skating fueled my passion for movement, expression, and a healthy competitive spirit for twenty-two years.

However, at the age of eight, I suffered a big blow. During a standardized test, the education system revealed deficiencies in my academic ability. I was diagnosed and labeled with a learning disability. Coming from a highly academic family, this was a major challenge to accept. My trusted teachers and administrators began to set boundaries and impose or project their limiting beliefs. They predicted I would have a mediocre educational experience and insisted college was doubtful. I began to face the fear and self-doubt of 'Am I good enough?' At a young age, I was forced to make a choice. Either I could believe the limitations and opinions of others, or I could reject the notion of boundaries. With the strength of my family behind me, I learned to become resourceful and find my best learning style. For every new challenge, I held no limitations about what I could achieve." (cont.)

K

"I navigated the education system with perseverance, making friends with my teachers and professors who became a supportive team of advocates. When I was accepted into the honors program at university, I put my nose to the grindstone and was determined to excel. I juggled a vibrant sorority social life while pursuing my passion for skating. I continued to study long and hard to achieve academic success and graduated on the dean's list. I earned a dual undergraduate degree, which allowed me to complete a full bachelor's in three years and pick the fashion school of my choice for a second degree. Four years, two degrees, and proving anything is possible when you want it.

I went on to write my own story as a young female in the C-suite. Landing highly coveted positions in the corporate world of consumer products. I spent thirty years building a career partnering with big legacy brands and influential leaders. With a love of learning MY *way instilled from childhood, I had developed an unwavering commitment to find a solution (and never give up). I had a passion for challenge and purpose to rise to great heights on the corporate ladder. So, at the age of forty-five, I set my sights on an executive MBA at the University of Chicago Booth School of Business. Just two months before the program began, I felt conflicted. Did I really need another degree to make the impact I envisioned?" (cont.)*

K

Korie Minkus

"After playing by the rules throughout my career, I decided to ignite my wild child. I made the bold decision to leave corporate, burn my black pantsuits, and begin an entrepreneurial journey on my own terms. My family was my greatest support system, and through their words, I learned the importance of advocating for self. I refused to buy into other people's belief systems about my abilities. Today, I teach business owners how to do the same."

K

Korie Minkus

Can you remember what you were downloading as truth between the ages of birth and eight years old? In school, it was probably basic math, spelling, the organization of the solar system. But what were you downloading from your family or the other people around you? What were *their* beliefs? In the book *The Four Agreements*, author Don Miguel Ruiz describes the "dream," the ancient Toltec term for our human experience. The Toltecs describe our beliefs as inherited from the "dream of the planet" or from the "dream of the other people." As children, we don't *agree* to believe the dream of the planet or the dream of the others; that reality is forced on us in our impressionable years. In *The Four Agreements*, they call this downloading of information our *domestication*. Yikes—

drastic, right? But accurate. We, as adults, have the ability to break the bonds of our domestication, discover who we truly are, and make new agreements with ourselves. We can form new beliefs.

"I had a subconscious samskara. In my early years, I downloaded that achieving and being pretty was a way to earn love. I had zero awareness of this samskara until I was in my thirties, and I still have to be aware of this belief today. All areas of my life played out in this groove. As a child I made straight As and was the president of the class and head cheerleader. I didn't realize I was trying to earn the love and attention of my parents. I would sacrifice hours in the gym and deplete my food to have a lean body. I didn't understand that being pretty didn't translate to being more lovable. And in business, I over-gave to my own employees, expecting them to revere me, but instead they took advantage. This samskara is a black hole, with no fulfillment. I had to bring awareness to the patterns and develop the new belief that I am lovable and I am loved for being me."

A

Ashley Black

Maybe a quick parable would help illustrate what we're talking about. In the book *This Is Water,* author David Foster Wallace tells a story of two young fish who are out for a swim. They come upon an elderly fish, who says in passing, "Morning, boys. How's the water?" The two young fish look at one another, and one of them says, "What the hell is water?" The story is a commentary on how we perceive the world around us: "[T]he most obvious, important realties," Wallace says, "are often the ones that are hardest to see and talk about." Like the fish who don't think to question the water they swim in, our beliefs about the world and about our own abilities and worth can be as pervasive as the air we breathe—or in the case of the fish, the water they swim in. When something is so big and all-encompassing, it's easy to take it for granted as *just the way things are.* It's easy not to ask questions.

Why bring up this story? Well, once again, it boils down to what we've been saying all along: awareness, awareness, awareness! Most of our limiting beliefs might have been instilled in childhood, but the good news is that you don't have to be a child to develop new thought habits. If you open yourself to new experiences, you can create new neural pathways and adapt to new ways of thinking, even as an adult. The first step to overcoming your limiting beliefs and embarking on new and meaningful high-vibrational adventures is to identify *what* limiting beliefs you may have, beliefs that you swim in, like fish in water.

It's no surprise that limiting beliefs are tightly linked with your vibration level, because the belief is tied to the emotion *surrounding* the belief. If you spent your childhood in a low-vibrational environment, you probably just thought that was normal. You could have accepted things like yelling, an attitude of lack, a victim mentality, or gossip as "just the way things are." It's just like the fish parable, but instead of water, you were swimming in low vibrations. Keep in mind, though, that even if your childhood was relatively high-vibrational, you can still have limiting beliefs. You could be domesticated to believe that excessive shopping is normal or that if the mom isn't a stay-at-home parent, that's bad.

> *"Limiting beliefs are a part of life, often inherited and passed down generationally. Learning how to recognize them and then 'act on them' are two different disciplines. It's like passion with no purpose. Get good at both, as it will guide you to new discovery and truth. To discover truth and address my limiting beliefs, I have committed to silent retreats where I can explore deep learning in meditation, movement, and self-exploration. This type of mental space gives me the opportunity to redefine and re-wire beliefs by separating myself from my ego mind. We are constantly committed to others, now it's time to BE...committed to yourself. As my friend and mentor Les Brown has told me, 'If you are not willing to risk, you cannot grow. And if you cannot grow, you cannot become your best. And if you cannot become your best, then what is there?'"*

You might be doing as much work as you can to overcome your limiting beliefs, but if you're surrounded by low-vibrational people, it's going to be pretty hard not to feel low-vibrational yourself. On the other hand, if you surround yourself with high-vibrational expanders, what a difference it makes to your self-esteem and your ability to overcome limiting beliefs! It's better to be alone than to be surrounded by limiting, low-vibrational people, and there are plenty of ways to increase your vibration level independently: You can raise your vibration through expansive activities like reading, artmaking, traveling, or watching documentaries (we highly recommend the Gaia network).

The annoying thing about limiting beliefs is that once you identify them, the reveal can be a little jolting and even upsetting, meaning the transition from "limited" to "growth" mindset is rarely a smooth one. And our hypermasculine culture only contributes to that upset: Hypermasculine culture prioritizes strength over vulnerability. Oftentimes our limiting beliefs have been stuffed deep down and covered up—bringing them to the surface to achieve conscious awareness can trigger the emotions that accompany some limiting beliefs such as shame or guilt, some of the lowest vibrational emotions there are.

But sometimes the opposite happens and you could be elated that you've identified the source of the limiting belief. Eckhart Tolle, author of *The Power of Now*, says that by bringing the source of these beliefs to light, you can neutralize them on the spot. Regardless of your immediate reaction to the reality of your limiting beliefs, the ultimate objective is to bring awareness to the belief so that you can transcend it. Once you've identified what may be keeping you from reaching your highest potential, you become open to the many different means of reshaping your thoughts.

"Limiting beliefs, made stronger by the negative memories that bind them, keep us in victim mode. We need to refuse to remain there for long. I'm one of the millions of children who grew up with an alcoholic parent which, unfortunately, led to a lot of limiting beliefs. I had a rocky start, and I ended up with the "disease to please." For many years, I didn't know how to set healthy boundaries. "No" wasn't a word in my vocabulary. I found myself always trying to fix things for others, which is how I'd derive value in myself. For me, recognizing my own intrinsic value has been essential in overcoming the childhood beliefs that kept me stuck. We all must recognize our pasts as part of the unique puzzle that makes us who we are. That doesn't mean you're to blame for any of the bad that happened to you—it just means that new grooves are waiting. Know your worth. Be patient and persistent. And never let anyone make you believe you're not good enough."

In the business world, mindset is now considered one of the most important differentiators between why some people thrive and others flounder. Stanford psychologist and author Carol Dweck was the first to identify what she termed "fixed" and "growth" mindsets. She found that people who have a "fixed mindset" believe their basic characteristics, like intelligence or talent, are unchangeable traits. On the other hand, people with a "growth mindset" approach the world in a very different way. Their curiosity and openness give them the ability to evolve and expand, because they believe their potential is limitless.

When we talked to the women in the WotB about limiting beliefs, many of them recognized pervading self-sabotaging thoughts—that little bitchy voice in your head that whispers, *Am I worthy enough? Am I smart enough?* We had an honest and heartfelt conversation with these women about fixed versus growth mindset, and many of them came to realize they had the power to reframe their perspectives and transform their lives. If you haven't already, we encourage you to join the WotB. We're here to help you break down your limiting perceptions and enhance your growth mindset.

There are many techniques to help you overcome limiting beliefs from NLP to hypnotherapy, which activates your dreamy theta brain waves to make your thoughts more pliable. Theta is the most effective brain wave in which to overcome limiting beliefs, because when you're in theta, your mind becomes sleepy and more vulnerable to new ideas. But if NLP and hypnotherapy aren't your thing, don't worry—you can begin changing your limiting beliefs all on your own, just by, well, practicing. It may not be glamorous, but the phrase "practice makes perfect" is a cliché for a reason. More on this in the next chapter.

"I had the good fortune to be trained and certified in NLP by Michelle Masters. I spent one full year flying between Chicago and San Francisco, one weekend a month, to be educated and taught by the best. Michelle guided me on how to identify fixed beliefs and revise the patterning to create meaningful outcomes. Unfortunately, traditional academic curriculum doesn't teach self-development and personal transformation. I encourage our readers to seek techniques, mentors, and instruction, to expand your mind based in freedom, not trapped in limitations."

Korie Minkus

Whatever you choose to do, the most important thing is to find what works for *you*. We'll warn you, overcoming limiting beliefs is not a one-and-done situation—if it were, our lives would be so much easier! A lot of our limiting beliefs are so deep-seated that it will take a *long* time and *lots* of effort to overcome them. But it's possible, and it happens every day. Healing is a lifelong process.

MOVEMENT #5: GROWTH OR FIXED?

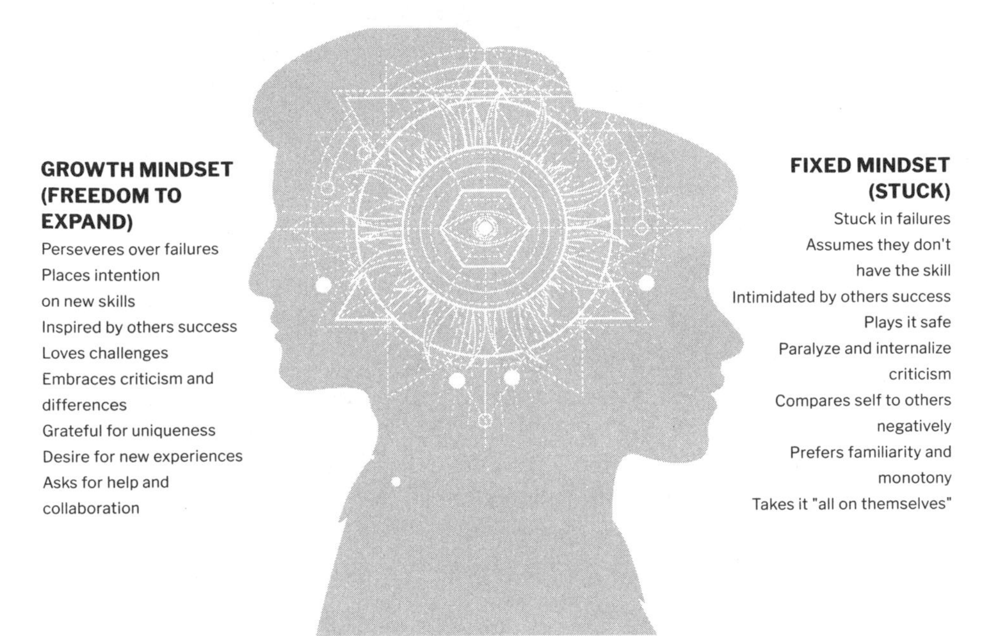

Take a few minutes to study the above chart. The attributes appearing in the list on the left reflect a mind that is expansive and unlimited, while the attributes in the list on the right reflect a mind that is low-vibrational and fixed. Go through each list and check off the attribute that best matches your mindset, and be honest! Do you embrace failure and learn from it, or do you avoid it and feel worthless because of it? Do you embrace challenges, or do you avoid them in favor of a more effortless life? Once you've checked off all of the attributes that best match your current mindset, tally them up: Do you have more checked items in the growth mindset column, or in the fixed mindset column?

"Growth and abundance bring a new sense of freedom. This discovery for me was an aha moment of possibility and hope. Many of us are preprogrammed that we go to school, get a degree, and work for someone forever to secure our financial freedom. That path leads to having only one source of income, and like me, living in fear of 'what if' that source of income is cut off. We are programmed to live under a false sense of control that others maintain in our life. As you expand your ability to embrace abundance, it becomes not just 'something for others.' It can open a maze of options. An example of this for me was when we hit a very challenging financial time during the global crisis in 2007. We had investments and lost over $1 million (yup, that is one hundred million pennies) and at the age of thirty-five, we were devastated. Plus, both my husband's and my financial livelihoods were being threatened. We had two children, and our fear was overcoming logic. At that time, we met a financial guru who taught us to broaden our view of how to create security and, at this very difficult time, focus on abundance over scarcity. Now, I am not suggesting money is the only form of abundance to achieve, but as Michelle Masters taught me, money is directly related to 'worth expansion.' The more you value your own worth, the more abundant money can become. This journey not only brought us a new sense of control in our purposeful lives, but it also taught us to not fear loss but instead to embrace it with abundance."

K

Korie Minkus

Regardless of where the majority of your checked boxes land, we suspect you have at least a few boxes checked in the fixed mindset list. What we'd like you to do now is take some time in the space below to address the fixed mindset boxes you checked, identify how this mindset affects your life, and come up with steps you might take to adjust your beliefs. We know—it's hard work. But living your most high-vibrational life is worth it.

Movement #5 Growth or Fixed?

Fixed Mindset Attribute	How does this attribute affect my life?	What steps can I take to adjust?

For your consideration

FOR YOUR CONSIDERATION: Take a few moments to reflect on the work you just did for this Movement. Look at the words you just wrote. What three words that you have added to the chart above ignite your passion the most? Write them here:		
1.	2.	3.

❁ CHAPTER SIX ❁

BE...Purposeful

Dr. Ona Brown

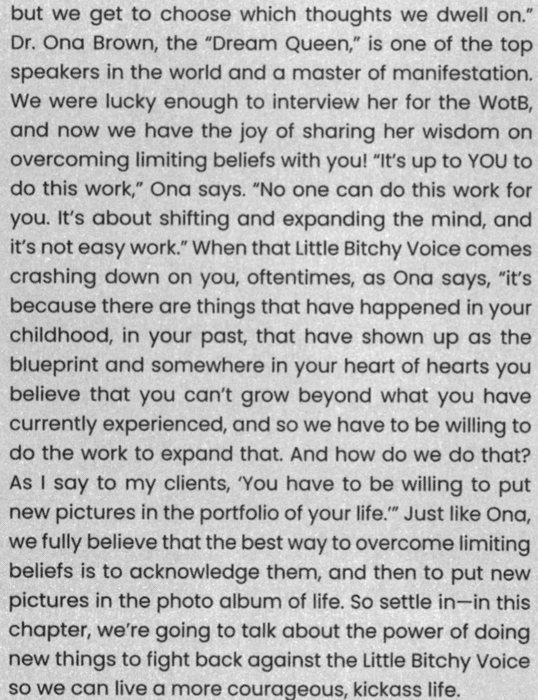

"We're gonna have low days," says Dr. Ona Brown, "but the reality is that even when we have low days, our lows can be *high* lows. We have negative thoughts, but we get to choose which thoughts we dwell on." Dr. Ona Brown, the "Dream Queen," is one of the top speakers in the world and a master of manifestation. We were lucky enough to interview her for the WotB, and now we have the joy of sharing her wisdom on overcoming limiting beliefs with you! "It's up to YOU to do this work," Ona says. "No one can do this work for you. It's about shifting and expanding the mind, and it's not easy work." When that Little Bitchy Voice comes crashing down on you, oftentimes, as Ona says, "it's because there are things that have happened in your childhood, in your past, that have shown up as the blueprint and somewhere in your heart of hearts you believe that you can't grow beyond what you have currently experienced, and so we have to be willing to do the work to expand that. And how do we do that? As I say to my clients, 'You have to be willing to put new pictures in the portfolio of your life.'" Just like Ona, we fully believe that the best way to overcome limiting beliefs is to acknowledge them, and then to put new pictures in the photo album of life. So settle in—in this chapter, we're going to talk about the power of doing new things to fight back against the Little Bitchy Voice so we can live a more courageous, kickass life.

instagram.com/ownwithona
facebook.com/OwnwithOna
twitter.com/OwnWithOna

MAKING NEW GROOVES

If you've stuck with us this far and managed not to crawl back into the comforting cave of your samskaras, we applaud you! Confronting limiting beliefs is tough, tough work. But it's not enough to just address the beliefs you've been cultivating since childhood; you also have to overcome them. And even then, if you smooth down the grooves in the record, the record won't play anything at all—you gotta carve out new grooves (or, as Dr. Ona Brown says, add new photos to the photo album). So we want to dedicate this chapter, the final in our Purpose section, to eradicating the old beliefs and practicing new ones. To smoothing down the record and making new grooves. Let that record spin, baby. Let your music play out, loud and clear.

As with most tasks, starting is often the hardest part. How do you just...make new beliefs? How do you suddenly become an open-minded person? The first (and, really, only) step is to *try something new and scary*. And when you've done that—do something *else* new and scary. And when you've done *that*... you get the picture.

As you go about your day, listen for that little voice that whispers, *What am I doing? This is a waste of time. I don't deserve this. I look ridiculous. I should be doing something else. I'm scared.* When you hear that voice—that's a *good sign*. That means you're doing something new, something that challenges your belief about your abilities, your worth, and the world around you. That little voice—the LBV, or Little Bitchy Voice—is a sign that you're on the cusp of a new adventure. So when you hear that little voice, ignore it, and enjoy the adventure. The more activities you do that trigger that little voice, and the more you continue doing the thing anyway, the more confident and expansive you will grow!

When you're in the middle of doing something and it sets off the LBV, in the moment, it's usually best to ignore the LBV and carry on doing what you were doing, if you can. But when you have the time to reflect, it's worth it to examine the limiting self-talk that you hear under specific circumstances. For instance, if you hear *You don't have the right clothes for that party* or *Nobody you know will be there*, is there a belief behind these statements that you can work to address, so that next time you find yourself in the same or a similar situation, the LBV will go away (or at least whisper more quietly)? Perhaps this self-talk is due to a conviction related to your self-worth—that you're too fat, too skinny, too poor, too uninteresting, what have you. By addressing this belief, you can work more specifically to overcome it. As you expand, as you keep trying new things and working to overcome your limiting beliefs, the LBV will pop up more and more, and we hope you'll take it as an opportunity to explore! When you explore the source of the LBV, you can become aware of your limiting beliefs and work to neutralize them.

When it comes to confronting your limiting beliefs and achieving success in life, the path is usually rocky and covered in brambles. If you "go easy" on yourself on this path, you'll never make it forward. Challenging yourself is a *must* if you want to live your best life. It sounds contradictory, but facing the things that trigger you is essential to healing from those things. Of course, when we tell you to get out of your comfort zone, we're not saying to ignore your safety—if you're in a dangerous or abusive situation, or when you need a moment to rest, take care of yourself! You should practice responding to your LBV on your own time and in your own way. Even if you do only one new thing every day, by the end of the year, you'll have done 365 things that have expanded the hell out of your comfort zone.

Ashley's example shows how to face your obstacles on your own steam. If you're feeling low or discouraged, this *isn't* a time to do something new or hard or face a trigger. It's kind of like this: When you break up with your boyfriend, that's not the time to chop off your hair (we've all been there!). First, work on your mindset and focus on self-soothing, self-love, and gratitude. Once you're in a higher-vibrational, more creative mood again, that's the time to go out and challenge that LBV! To put it in metaphorical terms, if your computer's operating system (OS) is running poorly, upgrading it might be impossible—it might not be able to handle all the latest and greatest software, and it'll crash. But if your OS is running well, it should be able to handle an upgrade, right? It's the same for people—when you're taking care of yourself and your energy can handle it, you're able to tackle new things, annoying things, limiting beliefs, challenging people, retraumatizing triggers. In short, you're able to "do the thing" that is outside of your samskaras.

So, when your tuning fork is vibrating at a high level and you're channeling your Divine Feminine, go out and ignite that Little Bitchy Voice. To make it easy on you, we've distilled all the steps to making new record grooves into one chart:

"I have great respect for my yoga philosophy teacher, Mariel. Each week she prays over our sessions and brings me insights and wisdom. As we were chatting, I told her how peaceful things had been lately and that I had been doing really well with detachment from heightened pleasure or pain. In her wisdom, she questioned me. She told me that I was living in paradise with the man I adored and not exposing myself to the very things that might bring up emotions. So as part of my 'work' for that week, I was challenged with the task of going into town and interacting with people who have a tendency to annoy me. She also challenged me to call certain people in my life that have a history of getting under my skin. I am happy to say that I was able to keep my indifference, but it was a great lesson about NOT only creating my high-vibrational external world, but also creating my high-vibrational inner world and a shield of my energy regardless of circumstance."

A

Ashley Black

EXPANSION WHEEL

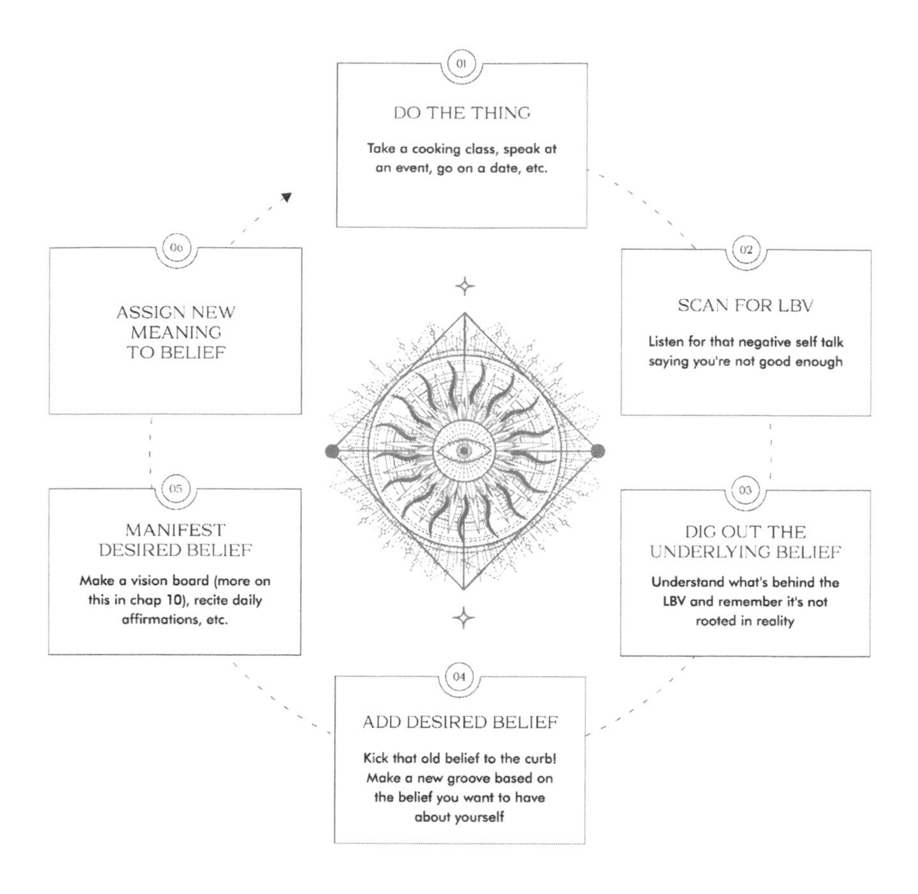

Notice the process ends right where it begins—at the scary thing. Like any real and lasting change, eradicating your limiting beliefs and living a more passionate and purposeful life is not a one-off thing, nor is it something you should ever stop. Most entrepreneurs will tell you, if you want to be a success in business, perseverance is key—you might even consider perseverance the silent fifth *P* in this book's title! You wouldn't think it, but perseverance is often more important than being smart, creative, or business savvy (though those are all important too, of course). As Einstein said, "It's not that I'm so smart, it's just that I stay with problems longer."

STOP waiting for the opportunity to live the life you want and MAKE the opportunity yourself. Don't wait for permission, give yourself permission! Take it from us, when you challenge that LBV enough to try new things, you're setting yourself up not only for a thriving and fulfilling personal life, but a thriving and fulfilling business life as well; all the greatest and most successful entrepreneurs base their personal brand and their product on living authentically and courageously in defiance of the Little Bitchy Voice! (We'll talk more about that in the next chapter!)

Changing your life is a slow process, but when you bring passion and purpose to your day-to-day, when you show up courageously each morning and show that LBV who's boss, your life as a whole will transform. And as cavalier as we might seem, challenging the LBV and reforming your samskaras is a lifelong process. You must show up each day prepared to bring your full passion and purpose to light.

MOVEMENT #6: EXPANSION WHEEL

For this Movement, we're going to ask you to make confronting that Little Bitchy Voice more than an abstract idea—we're going to ask you to make it a REALITY.

Look at the chart below. Seem familiar? We've taken the expansion wheel from this chapter and carved some space in it—space for YOU, where you can practice confronting your very own particular brand of LBV! Use one expansion wheel for each new thing you do to overcome a limiting belief. (You may want to begin on scrap paper, and then translate the basic ideas of your notes to the chart. We've added some blank space here for you, but feel free to record your thoughts in your journal or anywhere else before you input your thoughts into the chart.)

First, consider a scary activity that activates your LBV—say, speaking at a particular function about your business. Record the activity in the first bubble. Then, listen for the LBV: What is it saying to you about your abilities to speak well, or about the crowd's perception of you? Dig out that belief and explore what the root of it could be. Then, consider what beliefs you would like to replace it with instead: Is this a high- or low-frequency belief? After this, make a plan! How will you manifest this belief in your daily life? Lastly, what is the new meaning you can assign to this belief?

Once you have filled out the chart to reflect a specific activity, cut the chart out and tape it somewhere you'll see it often—in your planner, on your vanity mirror, on the coffee machine.... The more you look at it and stay aware of the LBV and its origins, the easier it is to overcome the limiting belief that has you spiraling and instill an empowering, high-frequency belief in its place!

We've given you six, so don't just do this exercise once—do it multiple times. Maybe multiples times in one day!

"My experiences in life and business enriched me with a profound, unshakable calling to protect and uplift women. I didn't always know how that purpose would play out, and it's led me down many different paths. I faced the LBV when I applied to law school, and again when I began a career as a storyteller and video producer. The LBV wouldn't shut up when I worked on my documentary Raising Humanity, *but I later won a Silver Telly award as the executive producer. The LBV resurfaced with a vengeance when I had cancer, but I squashed that bitch and came out stronger. In WotB, some women have shared with me that they don't know what they're good at. They're not sure where to start, let alone where to expand. We've all been there. I had to assign fresh meaning to my beliefs with every new chapter and every new step I took, and with each Movement, you can too."*

EXPANSION WHEEL

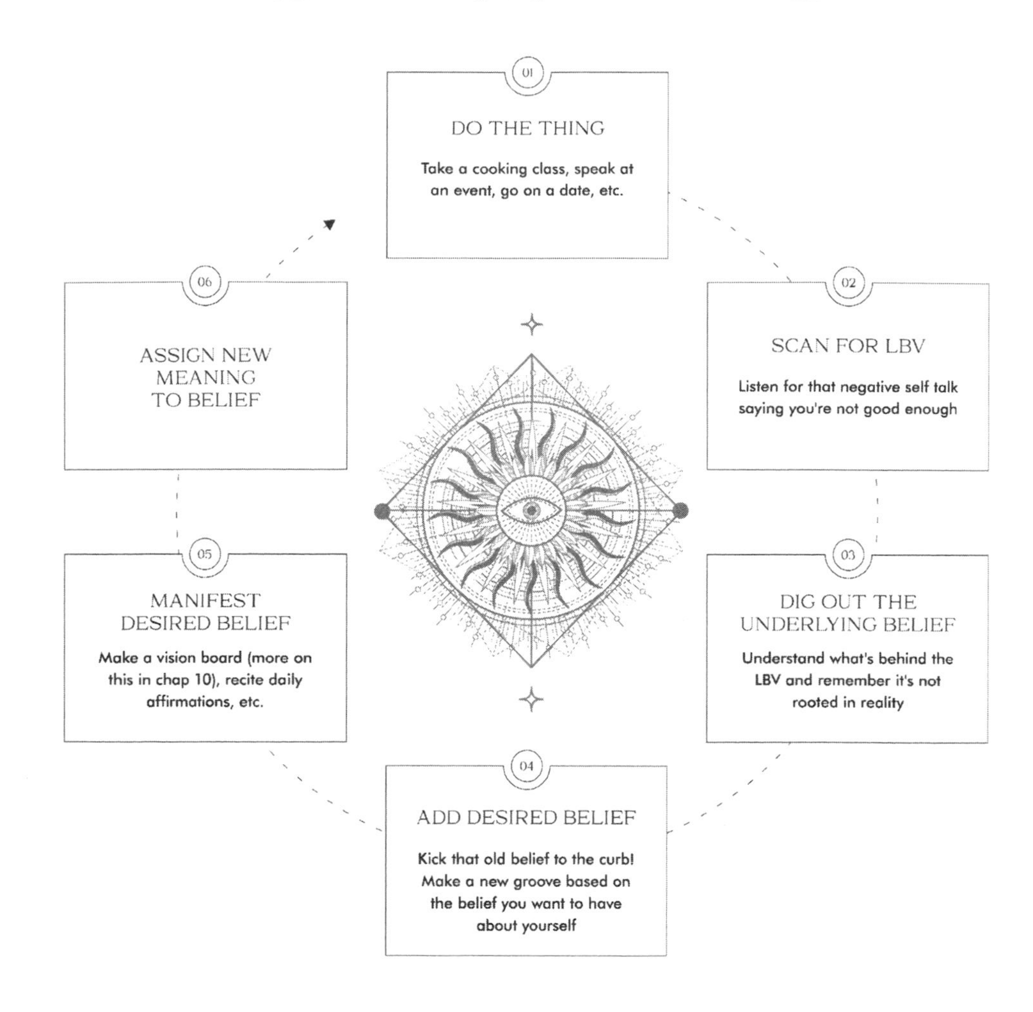

For your consideration

FOR YOUR CONSIDERATION: Take a few moments to reflect on the work you just did for this Movement. Look at the words you just wrote. What three words that you have added to the chart above ignite your passion the most? Write them here:		
1.	2.	3.

PART III

Products

❀ CHAPTER SEVEN ❀

BE...Personal

Julie D'Angelo

Christina Fontanesi

Creators of Detox Babe

Julie D'Angelo and Christina Fontanesi's entrepreneurial success is a testament to the power of the personal brand and the perseverance of the human spirit. Both women—still not yet thirty!—met in college and found their purpose after experiencing separate tragedies: While Christina underwent treatment for Lyme disease, her friend and roommate, Julie, suffered a sexual assault that shattered her sense of self-worth. These two beautiful young women took the hurdles life threw their way in stride, not only overcoming them, but using their experiences as the catalysts for a thriving business: Detox Babe, through which they sell bath products. As Christina healed from her painful disease, salt baths were the only thing that gave her relief; at the same time, as Julie worked to recover her sense of self, baths were an incredibly important component of her self-care practice: "[The bath] was a safe place in a world where I didn't feel safe," Julie says. "Sitting alone in a bathtub is a beautiful moment of relief and clarity that you can do for yourself. So we both just really dove in because of how good it made us feel for both situations we were going through, mentally and physically. And that turned into...creating this brand around [the idea], 'Let's help other people heal.' Because suffering is universal." Like Ashley and her personal history developing the FasciaBlaster, Julie and Christina's own self-care journeys ignited in them a passion to help other people experience the same healing, which naturally blossomed into a personal brand. We'll talk more about how to transition your passion and purpose into a personal brand in this chapter, so stick around. And if you would like to hear more about Julie and Christina's business, visit them here:

instagram.com/detoxbabe

PERSONAL BRANDING

Congratulations! You made it to the halfway point. This is so exciting, because there's some *j u i c y* stuff in this next part of the book. In this chapter alone, we're going to take all the material and hard work you did in the previous sections about living passionately and purposefully, and, to put it bluntly, we're going to help you parlay it into the cha-ching. We applaud the courage and determination Julie and Christina displayed in overcoming their obstacles and using their experiences in their entrepreneurial journey. Now we'd like to discuss how you too can leverage your passion and purpose into an authentic personal brand to lead you to products and prosperity. So get pumped as we transition into monetizing the product that is YOU.

One of the ways the Divine Feminine has been co-opted by hypermasculinity is that we tend to treat women who want to work or strive to be financially successful like "chicks with dicks"—mercenary and "unfeminine." Well, we are here to tell you these are lies, all lies! As much as we wish it weren't true, you need money to survive. Hell, you need money to treat yourself, too. We hope we've established that you don't need lots of money to live high-vibrationally, but the flip side of that idea is that there's also nothing *wrong* with having money: you're not spoiled or self-centered for making that paper, girl! The goal is FREEDOM. And financial freedom is just as important as freeing yourself from limiting beliefs and low vibrational emotions.

As we've been talking about for the last six chapters, making money without feeling fulfilled or living authentically is not going to lead to true prosperity, which we are going to talk much more about in the final chapters. Money, as they say, can't buy happiness. But you want to know what the funny thing is? Society tends to tell you that you have to choose between thriving in the workplace and being yourself, but in reality, you can be a more successful entrepreneur when you are living authentically and aligned with your true Divine Feminine nature. Shocking, right? We often think of "professionalism" as being shiny and flawless, error-free, wrapped up neatly with a bow. Well, studies actually indicate that most clients prefer a business that seems "human!" When the owner of a business or the inventor of a product engages with their client base in an authentic, human way, clients are more likely to do business with that person. In other words, you're not selling your product; you're selling *you*.

Though we three have years and YEARS of experience in the entrepreneurial world, we'll remind you that we aren't writing a how-to guide here. But if what you're after are the ins-and-outs of business, seminars, retreats, and other goodies—oh girly, we have it ALL online.) We're here now to talk to you about your approach to business—how to do it high-vibrationally and, above all, authentically. The world is waiting for your most authentic you! Which is where your personal brand comes in.

When we say "personal brand," we're referring to the ways in which you advocate for yourself, your values, your purpose, and your passion. Your personal brand is simply the outward expression of what's you on the inside, absolutely buzzing with authentic passion. Social media has become a ubiquitous and useful tool for personal branding (though it's not the only tool). What does your brand, online or off, say about you and what you believe? When you Google your name, what comes up? What do you *want* to come up (or to *not* come up)? What do you want to be known for or associated with? These are all questions to ponder as we move through this chapter.

Simon Sinek, in his famous TED Talk "Start with Why," explains that people buy from people who have the same beliefs. They buy because they believe what you believe. "I believe," Sinek rants in his talk, "I believe, I believe." To further emphasize his point, Sinek observes that Martin Luther King, Jr., said, "I have a dream," not "I have a plan." So your personal brand is all about what YOU believe and expressing that in words, colors, symbols, imagery, and, ultimately, a product or product line. It's time to share with the world what it is that you're all about, what you believe.

"My entire brand is my why: I do not want to see another person struggle with their health or appearance with the lack of knowledge of fascia. I believe there is a better way to take care of our bodies. I believe we can all be empowered to have the best fascia system possible, and hence a greater level of health. Every product, every marketing initiative, every blog, every social post make up my branding, and my branding is a reflection of my very passionate why. I represent my brand publicly, and I take to the airwaves unpolished, raw, and real. I have attracted a tribe of people who resonate with my message, and I tell it like it is. Real people are starving for real people and, therefore, authentic brands. I wouldn't have over six million people following me if I didn't give them the real-deal Ashley, with a real-deal message and a real-deal brand."

Ashley Black

Sinek best sums up the importance of personal branding with his "Golden Circle" theory, which appears in the chart below. To paraphrase Sinek's words, most people approach the circle from the outside: "Every business knows *what* they do; most know *how* they do it; but very few know *why* they do it. And the ones that start from the inside-out—the ones that know why, the ones that *start* with why—those are the innovators, the geniuses, the ones ahead of the curve." So think of your personal branding as your *why*: rather than starting with what your product *is* or *should be*, ask yourself, "Why am I doing this? Why is the world the way it is (and how can I contribute)?" or, as Sinek says, "What is your purpose? What's your cause? What's your belief? [...] Why do you get out of bed in the morning? And why should anyone care?" Your personal brand is your expression of the passion and purpose you have worked so hard to develop in the earlier chapters. You're now ready to take on your own golden circle and express your brand to the world.

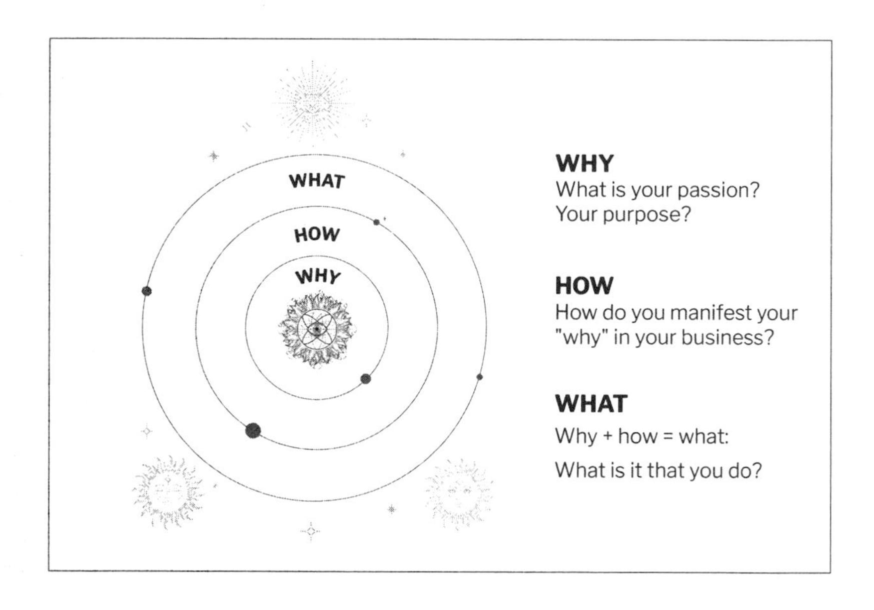

"I've supported hundreds of people on their entrepreneurial journeys. For many years, I've channeled my passion and purpose through the art of visual storytelling. My passion is to mentor women from all walks of life to stand in their power, and my purpose is to give them the tools and frameworks to communicate their truths. Video has been the how *fueling my* why. *Coco Chanel once said, 'The most courageous act is still to think for yourself. Aloud.' I couldn't start helping others find their voices until I found mine. On the road to elevating other women, I had to learn how to elevate myself in a way that was recognizable to others who would truly see me. I had to channel my past to light my present and ignite my future. Give yourself permission to speak your truth and be vulnerable. I had to come out from behind the camera and reveal who I really am. Your personal experience is your wisdom. When I learned to speak from my heart without caring what anyone would think, I found the courage to take my place, center stage."*

L

Lisa Vrancken

When you're vibrating at your highest, most fulfilled level, when you're aglow with passion, when your purpose is fueling the fire—what's your *why*? If you do not have a fully developed cohesive brand immediately, that's okay, it's all part of the journey. If you continue to refine your brand by living authentically and embracing your Divine Feminine energy, the *why* will come. And if you are well-rooted in your passion and purpose, we invite you to leave the door open for even more expansion.

MOVEMENT #7: GOLDEN CIRCLE

OK ladies, you're ready, you're authentic, you're passionate, you're oozing with purpose. Now it's time to get your brand on. We love Simon Sinek's Golden Circle theory—so much so that we've built an entire Movement around it. We hope this exercise will get your personal branding juices a-flowin'.

We'll confess: We've been a little sneaky. If you're observant, you might have noticed we asked you at the end of each Movement leading up to this one to identify the three words or ideas from each Movement you filled out that ignite your passion and set your heart ablaze and record them. For this Movement, we are going to ask you to flip back to those pages and assemble the words you have collected. Rewrite your words from the last six chapters in the spaces below, just so we have them all in one place:

Movement #7 Golden Circle

Chapter 1:	Chapter 2:	Chapter 3:
Chapter 4:	Chapter 5:	Chapter 6:

Why have we been asking you to do this after each Movement? Let us explain: It can be hard to describe your personal brand when you feel on the spot—which makes sense, because your personal brand (i.e., *YOU*) is something that develops organically over time; nothing authentic was ever formed instantaneously or under pressure. This is why we've been quietly asking you to record the words and ideas that you felt passionately about in the previous chapters—so that you could identify aspects of your brand organically and over a period of time and through careful reflection. Now, after six chapters of recording the words that ignite your passion, you have a garden of ideas to pull from as you navigate filling out your own Golden Circle.

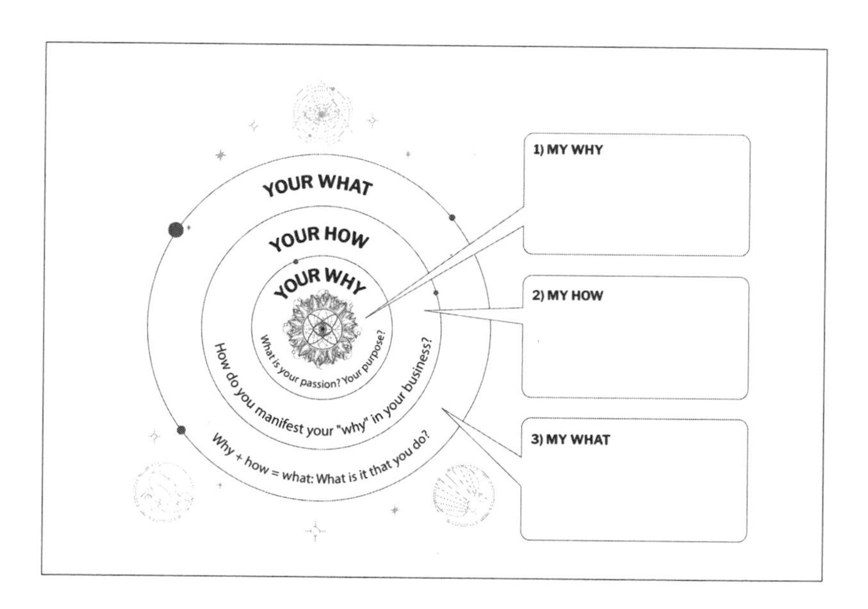

CHAPTER EIGHT

BE...*Innovative*

Sonia Laguna

At the age of thirty-nine, Sonia Laguna experienced major upheaval; her daughter died in a car accident, and her Häagen-Dazs franchise went under. Her savings were gone, and she felt it was too late to return to the corporate world. "I was a wounded puppy with no passion or purpose. I didn't know what to do, so I went back to what I was good at: consulting manufacturers in the Latin American market." Aimless, Sonia eventually decided to take a chance on a promising young Brazilian collagen vendor, who was having trouble getting his product, Qualinova, into the US: "Despite the challenges, I knew a golden opportunity when I saw one. I told him, 'I want to invest in your product.'" This venture required hard work and dedication, but by using what resources she had and using them wisely, Sonia was able to amass a market for her product: "We had hundreds of orders and a community that was excited about the brand with very little marketing. I decided that if our biggest problem was bringing our product into the country, then I was going to figure out a way to make it happen.... Because we were selling directly, we had very little overhead and a larger margin to play with. We were able to absorb that cost, and we haven't stopped selling since." Talk about pivoting! Sonia's life came to an unexpected

jolt when her world fell apart on the cusp of age forty. But she kept going and found a new path that aligned with her authentic self. "The life of an entrepreneur is not for everyone. I'm a high-risk personality. It's how I'm wired. Everything in life is a risk, but I always choose to bank on myself." You tell 'em, Sonia! In this chapter, we're going to talk about the many different business models you might consider adopting in your own entrepreneurial life. But whether you follow a path similar to Sonia's or carve one out all on your own, we hope you'll bank on yourself.

instagram.com/myqualinova

PICKING YOUR PRODUCT

Now all that talk about the importance of personal branding isn't to say that *what* you're selling isn't important—the opposite, in fact! If your entrepreneurial success depends at least somewhat on your ability to be authentic, then you have to make sure your product is 1. something you are **passionate** about and something others will be passionate about, and 2. something that brings you a sense of **purpose** that others may share or that might contribute to the greater good. This is simply aligning with your market. It's also important to attract your market through manifestation and vibration. (It's all coming together now, right?)

On a basic level, all you really need to do in order to identify or expand your product(s) is to keep cultivating your personal brand, and things will fall into place. Even if you're a seasoned entrepreneur already, this is still the key for your product. But if you're looking for a "simple" way to figure out what your product should be or how to expand, consider the ikigai. In the groundbreaking book *The Blue Zones* by Dan Buettner, he identifies eight areas of the world where the life expectancy is a hundred years and observes the common characteristics of the cultures. One such place is Okinawa, Japan. And one such characteristic that led to longer and happier living is what the Japanese call the ikigai, which might be simply understood as a "reason for being." All Blue Zone cultures have their version of ikigai, and for good reason—it brings passion, purpose, and prosperity together for "successful living." This chart breaks it down in an easy-to-understand way:

Look closely, and you will see that if one of those ingredients is missing, the plan is destabilized: A product without passion leaves you empty; a product for which the world has no need leaves you abandoned and uncertain. The thing about developing a product is that it goes beyond simply applying intention to your acts, as we discussed in chapter four. When translating your purpose to the business world, you might consider what needs there are in the world and how you can apply your passion and purpose to fulfilling those needs. The path might not always be linear, but when everything in this chart is in alignment, things sort of fall into place! The universe will broaden the path for you.

The purpose of this book is about inspiring you to approach business in a high-vibrational way. We want to help you figure out how to live authentically and in alignment with the Divine Feminine so that you will have the strength to persevere as an entrepreneur and to enjoy the process. (And, quite frankly, we want to teach you how to keep yourself in check all along the way!) Though our hypermasculine society discourages engaging with the Divine Feminine in the entrepreneurial world, we think you'll find that the more you channel your feminine attributes—like curiosity, collaboration, and creativity—the more easily the details of running your business will unfold! We're often conditioned to believe these feminine qualities will inhibit entrepreneurial success, but, in fact, engaging your Divine Feminine energy can help to remove a LOT of the guesswork involved in launching and sustaining your business.

All that being said, this chapter is meant to expand your horizons when considering your product suite. We have featured countless successful entrepreneurs with powerful personal brand stories on our weekly podcast; these entrepreneurs have all picked their product(s) for different reasons. From inventing a product to improving on what's already out there to distributing something you love, there are many other ways to bring a product to market. Whatever path you choose, the journey begins with you.

INVENTING A PRODUCT

Inventing a product is the hardest of the three to do, *and* the easiest one to explain. When you invent a product, you identify a need in the world that you're passionate about addressing, respond to it, and identify a gap in the current market where you and your product will be well received. Inventing is arguably the most creative form of entrepreneurship—it is laced with Divine Feminine characteristics and highly fulfilling. But keep an eye on your attachment to the outcome, because inventing is risky business; the more you attach to a specific outcome, the less flexible you become, and the more likely you are to be disappointed or feel like a failure. Pivoting is essential in business—especially when it comes to the high-risk world of inventing.

We've made a little pros and cons chart to help illustrate just what we mean by the "risks" of inventing—but there are plenty of rewards, too.

When you invent your own product, it's your baby. You created it, you cared for it, you patented it.... OK, I guess that's where the baby metaphor falls apart. Anyway, creating your own product is the most personal connection you can have to your business. But there are risks inherent in that, too: getting a product you've invented off the ground is...expensive. And slow. And HARD. We can talk about personal branding until the cows come home, but getting people to rally around your product is often a long, slow, pricey process. And, because inventing your own product *is* so personal, if your venture falls flat of your expectations, the pain might feel more dramatic. But if your venture succeeds—*look out, world!* When you invent, patent, and successfully launch a product or product suite, the sky is really the limit. You're unique. You will be bountiful with passion and purpose. You'll get the credit for being the inventor, and if you decide to exit, you can sometimes get good multiples for your inventions. This is usually not the case if you improve or distribute. So this is the encouragement: go for it, but know what you're signing up for. High risk, high return.

INVENTING A PRODUCT

PROS	CONS
Usually patentable/ Creative control	Risky
Uniqueness and personal connection	Expensive
No cap on potential	Slow to market

"When I invented my inaugural product, the FasciaBlaster, it was a passion project. I wanted to use the tool in my sports medicine clinics. When I made the connection with cellulite, I thought maybe I could have mass-market success. I manufactured the molds and ordered one thousand units in 2010. It took me over six years to sell the first thousand, and I was hundreds of thousands of dollars of my own, hard-earned money in. I maxed every credit card and got any type of loan someone would give me. I remember thinking for years, 'When is the money going to come?' I had celebrities and doctors raving about my product and I knew it worked. I was known as one of the best body workers. But the money took a long time; I had to work my 'day job' double the amount of time to fund my life AND the FasciaBlaster. It was a brutal road of day-in and day-out grind for six years, and it cost a LOT of dough, but once I came over the hill, the pot of gold was actually there at the end of the rainbow. I got my break in 2016 and 2017 with the introduction of Facebook ads and did over $40 million that year. Ads were not the magic bullet—my perseverance was."

A

Ashley Black

IMPROVING ON A PRODUCT

Maybe we've sufficiently shined a light on the potential downsides of inventing with our talk about its risks. Or maybe you just don't have that million-dollar idea (yet!). Or maybe you're looking around at all the gadgets and services people are going nuts for and crossing your arms and saying, "*Pffft.* That old thing? *I* can do better than *that.*" Then maybe your future lies in improving an existing product. More than thirty thousand new consumer products are launched each year and, according to Nielsen, 70 percent are actually just tweaks or updates on an existing design.

When we talk about improving a product, we mean just what we say: You see a product that's already out there, and maybe the product is even thriving (and that saves you a lot of marketing footwork!), but *you* can see room for improvement. Remember how we talked about finding that gap in the market when you're inventing a product? It's the same thing with modifying an existing product: find the gap in an already existing business and crawl into it. If you can take an existing product and make it better-looking, better-functioning, faster, easier, or less expensive...boom, you're in the slot! Less money upfront. Less market education. Less time to develop. The downside is that you've now established yourself as the competition.

The world of product improvement can also encompass white-labeling. This is where the manufacturer of the product will allow you to make improvements and distribute the product as if it's your own. This could be minor alterations to the product and big alterations to packaging. For example, your personal brand might align with self-care products like candles. Maybe you want specific scents that reflect your mission. You don't have to start pouring candles in your garage and patenting the methodology. You simply have to find white-label candles that smell the way you want them to. Or you work with the manufacturer to make your custom scent. Then you can pick your own packaging, you can come up with creative names, you can make them in interesting sizes and shapes, and effectively *make it your own*. You didn't invent the candle, but you're putting your own spin on it.

Let's take a peek at the some of the high-level pros and cons of improving an existing product:

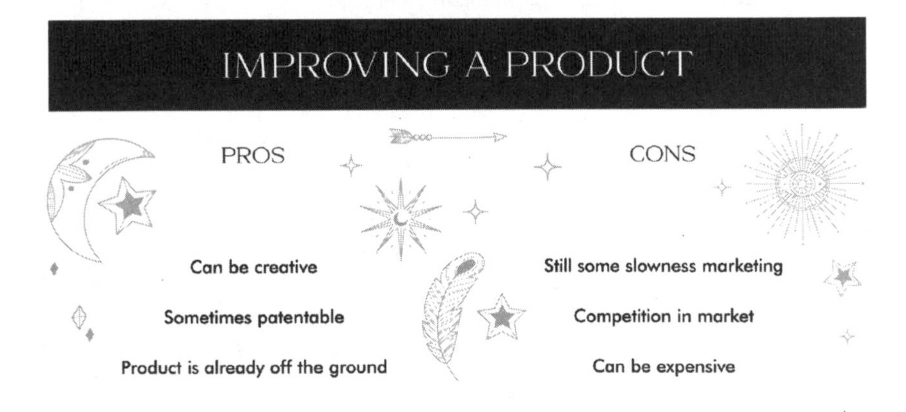

Of course, improving a product isn't easy, either, and just as with inventing a product, there are some cons. You're piggybacking off someone else's product, which might make things easier and still allow room for creativity, but it's a lot less personal than creating the product yourself. And though your product is already off the ground, there still might be some market competition to battle—but if your modifications are good enough, you'll cut down that competition in no time. This is a great model for the inventor-at-heart type, with less budget.

"An example of this is my client Paola Shah, the founder and CEO of Tucketts. After helping a friend launch a Pilates studio, Paola researched and discovered inspiration to free the toes in socks. Her passion was to provide a better grip sock for barefoot activities and allow a foot-brain connection that empowers calm, certainty, and security. In 2014, Paola patented an 'improved version of a sock' that allowed the toes to stay engaged, create a sensory contact with the ground, and help strengthen the foot muscles, preventing injuries.

Paola's priorities for her product included engaging a manufacturing partner that embraced a clean product agreement and sustainable practices. She is committed to decreasing unemployment in South America, with a factory that is committed to deliver the highest-quality sock experience in the market. Paola came to Rock Your Product® during a time of desired growth and expanded market impact, seeking a new level of business acumen. As Paola says, 'a successful business is a combination of taking fearless steps in a personal and professional level.' (cont.)

> *"She thrived in our program and was provided very strategic, direct steps to expand. Today, Tucketts is named the best gripper sock in the market and has been featured in* Shape *and* Women's Health *magazines. Now as a seven-figure business owner, Paola was recently honored by Goldman Sachs investment banking company for her entrepreneurial journey as a Latino woman and an inspiration for other aspiring female business owners."*

K

Korie Minkus

DISTRIBUTING A PRODUCT

The third way of bringing product to the market is through distribution. Distributing a product is basically marketing a product(s) and tracking shipments. Distributors may not get to be as creative or as involved in developing a product as inventors, but you bet your ass distribution is essential to most businesses' success; simply put, the more accessible your product is, the more people will buy it. For example, our friend, Shelda Magistri, founder of Brain Health Sciences, is a professional distributor with a vast network. When she discovered the Brain Tap—a headset and an app that helps balance brain waves—she fell in love with it (and so did we, by the way). This product aligned perfectly with Shelda's vision and values and authentic self. She was able to leverage her network and get special distribution rights for the product. *Voilà!* It's an instantaneous way to start a business. Distributing is a great way to make the product your own by *skipping* the inventing and manufacturing.

It's also worth mentioning that the world of affiliate marketing is EXPLODING right now. **Affiliates** are people who earn money by advertising a company's products and taking a commission on every sale they make. Thanks to social media, "regular folk" as well as celebrities and influencers can get in on the financial action of brands they want to promote. You've probably seen products advertised by affiliates in the form of social media posts or in listicles advertising the Top Ten Best Eye Creams of 2022: these ads are often accompanied by an "in paid partnership with." Affiliate marketing is one of the fastest growing jobs, and it's easy to get involved, meaning almost anyone can get a piece of a product's pie, from inventors to improvers to distributors and marketers. Almost all brands have an affiliate model, no matter the size of the audience, and there is no upfront cost to be an affiliate.

However you approach the distributor model, distribution is great for entrepreneurs with less risk tolerance. Let's check out some more pros and cons:

Distribution requires very low startup costs in comparison to inventing or improving on a product, and many distributors maintain a flexible schedule, working only twenty or thirty hours per week. So if you'd like to invent a product or work on modifying an existing product but aren't ready to take the plunge yet or want a backup plan, distributing might offer you the flexibility and security to work on other projects as a side-hustle. Or maybe you find fulfillment in distributing alone, and you can dedicate the rest of your time to your personal life. It doesn't really matter—as long as you believe in what you're doing and why you're doing it, the pieces will fall into place. (More about designing your ideal work/life balance in the last three chapters!)

We wrote this section knowing that we have women that already run seven-, eight-, and nine-figure businesses, as well as women who aren't at that stage but who have the entrepreneurial twinkle in their eye. These business models are all great ways to participate in commerce, but by no means are you limited to one model only. In fact, Ashley's product suite encompasses all three models. She has her inventions, the FasciaBlaster tools and some other things; her oils and creams are improvements; and her supplements and clothing are examples of distribution models. She is even an affiliate for Sunlighten saunas and other products she believes in.

Whether to invent, improve, or distribute isn't an either/or situation, it's a "spinning plate" scenario. Which plates do you wanna throw up in the air and why? Does what you're doing align with your risk tolerance and timeline? We encourage you to approach these models from an authentic place, with eyes wide open about what your needs are. It's all about pacing your time and your budget and balancing it with your goals. No matter where you are in the journey, each of these ways of doing business can enhance your product business.

MOVEMENT #8: INNOVATION BRAINSTORM

We hope this chapter has shed some light on the myriad different means of beginning or expanding your business and maybe given you an idea of what sort of venture is the right one for you. For this Movement, we'll continue exploring entrepreneurship through inventing, improving, and distributing with a little brainstorming...and a little *make-believe*. Let your sweet, alpha-child self shine!

For the first part of this exercise, we'll ask you to record an idea for **a product or product suite you would like to invent, improve on, or distribute/market**—or, if your business is already well under way, an idea for an **enhancement** you can make to your business or a **new product or product suite** you would like to take on, either as inventor, improver, or distributor. Maybe you already have a slew of ideas, or maybe you've never really thought much about it before! Take the space below to fill in the details of your product:

Movement #8 Innovation Brainstorm

What is your product or product suite called? Describe it---—what does it do? What purpose does it serve?
Is this product an original invention, a product you're improving on, or a product you're distributing/marketing?
Think back to your Golden Circle from Movement #7. How does this product or business venture reflect your Why, How, and What?
OK, we're gonna get a little artsy here! Draw your dream product logo!

We hope you had some fun with this exercise, and while we kept it light, it's our goal to help you explore your options and figure out what works for you as an entrepreneur and as a woman. Maybe you flew through this exercise because you knew *exactly* what you wanted to do, or maybe you moved slowly, taking every possible outcome into consideration. Either path is valid, as long as it's *yours.*

❁ CHAPTER NINE ❁

BE...Primed

Charmane Andrews Skillen

Founder and CEO, s.a.l.t. sisters

We recently spoke to Charmane Andrews Skillen, founder and CEO of s.a.l.t. sisters, in the WotB about her organic entrepreneurial journey from stay-at-home mom to cooking teacher to major player in the salt retail industry: "My business was born out of a passion for a healthy lifestyle and my love of cooking. As a stay-at-home mom, my focus was on raising my four daughters and keeping my family as healthy as possible for many years. When my youngest turned eighteen, I felt a pull to do something more with the knowledge and leadership skills that I had honed. I had started teaching cooking classes in an upscale farmers market, and when they encouraged me to create a retail presence, I decided I was going to sell salt." Charmane's personal branding, born of her passion for health and the sense of purpose she found in cooking for others, meant her path to salt retail was a natural one, even though nobody else saw it at first: "Everybody thought I was crazy, but it was a perfect extension of the health journey I had been on with my family and my belief in the foundational importance of food in our daily lives.... As an entrepreneur, you desire to impact other people through your products. There's all this momentum pushing you for-

ward. The hard part is staying true to yourself and not letting mistakes pull you down." Just like Charmane, we value prioritizing YOUR needs—your passions and your energies—above expectations about what you "should" do. In this chapter, we're going to talk about how to launch and scale your business according to YOUR vision of success. Stick around.

instagram.com/charmane_andrews_skillen
Saltsisters.net

LAUNCHING AND SCALING YOUR BUSINESS

Entrepreneurs build businesses out of ideas. Female entrepreneurs are special, because our product ideas are often based in emotional connection, intuition, and the desire to create abundance—all attributes of the Divine Feminine. Women nurture by nature, and our innovations have brought joy to many—just like Charmane's salt! For these reasons, female entrepreneurs are now the fastest growing category of change-makers worldwide.

Unfortunately, there's still some women who give up before bringing their ideas to life. It's those damn limiting beliefs. Even when we think we're over it, they come back to haunt us. We hear it all the time: *I'm not smart enough. I don't have the time. I'm too old. Nobody cares. I don't know how. I'm afraid.* Women also express feeling too paralyzed to move forward with an idea, because they don't know what steps to take to turn ideation into action. This applies not only to burgeoning entrepreneurs but established ones as well. (We can tell you from our experience, that Little Bitchy Voice doesn't ever completely go away!) What can an entrepreneur do when an idea pops into her head that she's not sure what to do with? How does she know if the idea is good enough to succeed? How does she budget her time and money wisely? Remember, if you have a business idea you'd like to develop, we're here in the WotB to help you determine if it's viable. But there are simple and straightforward steps you can take to assess your idea and how to put it into action.

Like we said, this book isn't a step-by-step guide to starting a business. It is, above all, a book about how to channel your Divine Feminine energy in your personal and professional lives to achieve prosperity—however you define "prosperity." For Charmane, her salt business is a natural extension of her passion for healthy living. For you, it's...who knows?! You decide! We would like to dedicate this chapter to a guide not for getting your product or product suite off the ground, but for maintaining control of your authentic Divine Feminine self as you navigate the tumultuous waters of entrepreneurship (or, if you're already swimming those waters, how to stay afloat!).

There are endless ways to launch and scale your business. Whether you opt for paid ads or social media promotion, online marketing, or keep it old-school, like a lemonade stand, self-distribute or outsource to another company, there isn't any *wrong* way to do things, as long as you keep doing *your* thing. But how do you know what's right for you? How do you decide which option makes the most sense for you *right* here, *right* now, with all the resources you currently have?

"After working with CEOs, founders, and entrepreneurs on emerging and Fortune 500 brand growth over three decades, in 2017 I packaged together the lessons learned, failures experienced, and winning tools to launch and scale a product business. With my proprietary system called Rock Your Product®, we have advised and mentored over one hundred thousand businesses globally in these distinctions. For both our private clients and group training programs, we deliver a customizable sequenced roadmap to avoid the posers, dishonesty, misguided information, and deception in business. This comprehensive end-to-end method from pre-revenue to mass market distribution provides the business acumen to avoid the landmines and make confident decisions. As a team, our distinguished board of advisors, consultants, and trainers have been featured on CNBC, Fox Business, Forbes, and Entrepreneur *magazine in expertise ranging from operational mastery, marketing and category leadership, sales distribution channel growth, and asset development. We have been named the number one global product advisory and growth training company and have generated life-changing financial multipliers for our clients. My passion and purpose, at this stage in my journey, is to invest in conscious business owners ready to evolve their product idea into a rock-star brand."*

If you'd like to know more about different marketing and distribution styles, from dropship to marketplace, or the pros and cons of online versus offline marketing, make sure to check out WotB! There are literally hundreds if not thousands of ways to launch and scale products. Every week in the Writing of the Book we interview entrepreneurs from all stages of the game, and what we can tell you is that there is no silver bullet for success. Each product journey is unique, and we recommend working with a mentor, advisor, or consultant who can help you navigate the path to avoid the land mines. And even within that journey, the timeline is unique. So, as always, we invite you to our social media for our weekly discussions and personalized advice!

We invite you to consider where your time, energy, and money are going as you travel the entrepreneurial path. It's prudent to take stock of your abilities, expectations, and authentic vision for your entrepreneurial life, not just when you're first launching your business, but regularly as you travel the path, because life is ever-changing.

DO I GIVE A FU@$?

One thing to keep in mind is that as your business expands, and the greater and more numerous your responsibilities become, the more you may be forced to delegate some of your tasks to others—third-party distributors, affiliate marketers, personal assistants, and on and on and on. We often think of, say, CEOs of multimillion-dollar companies as being all-powerful, when the reality is the more business their company does, the more they have to let go of what we call "the sausage-making." You're not going to be in the back of the factory, watching each ingredient be sourced or the sausage be stuffed, you're going to be high-level, making partnerships with grocery stores and negotiating manufacturing deals. Little by little, the more energy you wish to claim (or reclaim), the more control you must cede. In short, it's all about shifting energy into collaboration and giving up the sausage-making.

We know your business is your baby. But it takes a village to raise a child. So ask yourself: How much energy do you have? How much do you want to retain? How much responsibility for your baby will you give others, and how much does your intuition tell you to hold on to? As your business grows and your responsibilities grow with it, your attention will stretch thinner and thinner, and as your attention spreads thin, there's potential for your authenticity to spread thin, as well. And above all else, we don't want to see you flashing fake smiles or phoning in your passion for your product. No matter how big your business grows, you can still rock your most authentic and high-vibrational self. It comes down to leadership; if expansion and growth are what you truly desire in your business, focus your efforts on building a team that believes what you believe and functions as an extension of you and your brand.

Just as important as asking yourself how much control you can and should give up is asking yourself, *Do I give a fu@$?* Believe us—it's real easy to be swept up in the growth of your business. When the opportunities come, you will innately want to pursue them all. BUT, one of the main points of this book is to bring mindfulness to your business choices. We are going to hand you an imaginary magic wand to wave over the opportunities and say, "Opportunity, opportunity on the wall, who's the fairest of them all?" In other words, do you really give a fu@$ about the thing you are investing energy into? Do you have the bandwidth to do it well, or is the timing wrong? Do you even have the desire to spend your time and energy on a specific part of your business? Use the "Do I give a fu@$?" approach when deciding what, who, and when—deciding to control, collaborate, or surrender.

"Every single day I am faced with the Do I give a fu@$? *scenario. It's amazing how often the answer is* No, actually, I don't give a fu@$ about that, *even though it may be a great money-maker or reputation-builder. I also stay out of the sausage-making of everything on the back end of my company, such as warehouse, fulfillment, wholesale, funding, etc. It's not that I don't want it done correctly—I collaborate with my team and have monthly check-ins—what I don't give a fu@$ about is doing that stuff myself. But the flipside is that I do things that aren't considered CEO or high-level, such as my own Instagram posts. I do them all myself because* I do give a *fu@$ that I personally represent myself—authentically. My point? The beauty of owning your own business is you get to decide. When to say yes, when to say no, when to say maybe later. Poof—magic."*

Ashley Black

Even though this isn't a step-by-step guide to launching your own business, we'd be remiss if we pretended that money didn't matter as you ask yourself what your business goals and options are. So, how do you keep track of your energy and your authentic vision on a budget that suits your life? You deserve to have money, choice, and opportunity. Yet, many women can still underestimate their worth. We encourage you to seek expertise in financial planning, regardless of how good you may be at the books: Seek out organizations, associations, or consultants that can provide you with access to greater financial education and independence. Get comfortable with budgeting, tracking, forecasting, investment fundamentals, and risk management. Surround yourself with people who have a high level of financial literacy and a strong abundance mindset to share. There's wisdom in the adage: "If you don't know your numbers, you don't know your business." Proudly project your nerdiness. Set time aside to regularly review your numbers. Engage professionals who can help you with financial strategies, accounting, tax planning, and investing your cash. With full confidence and capabilities, you will rule your financial world. This is the section where we have to "preach" a little bit, but we're not leaving you high and dry. This is where our community and social media can provide support, letting us vet and help guide you on your journey.

"There are so many women aching for someone to believe in their dreams. We formed BE...PPPP, LLC, with my co-authors Ashley and Korie to provide guidance, support, and love to every female entrepreneur. There's still work to be done, and every woman is in a different place in their journey. BE...PPPP, LLC, plans to offer self-transformational gatherings, professional masterminds, and retreats in Costa Rica and other exotic locations around the globe. We'll also be creating online courses to easily learn everything you'll need as a woman embarking on entrepreneurship."

L

Lisa Vrancken

The first step to getting your idea(s) underway is not always clear. To help you ask yourself the right questions without being prescriptive with the answers, we've developed a flowchart that addresses the concerns you might have regarding the launching and scaling of your business, whether you're just starting out or are in the thick of it and wondering how to move forward:

BUSINESS DEVELOPMENT WHEEL

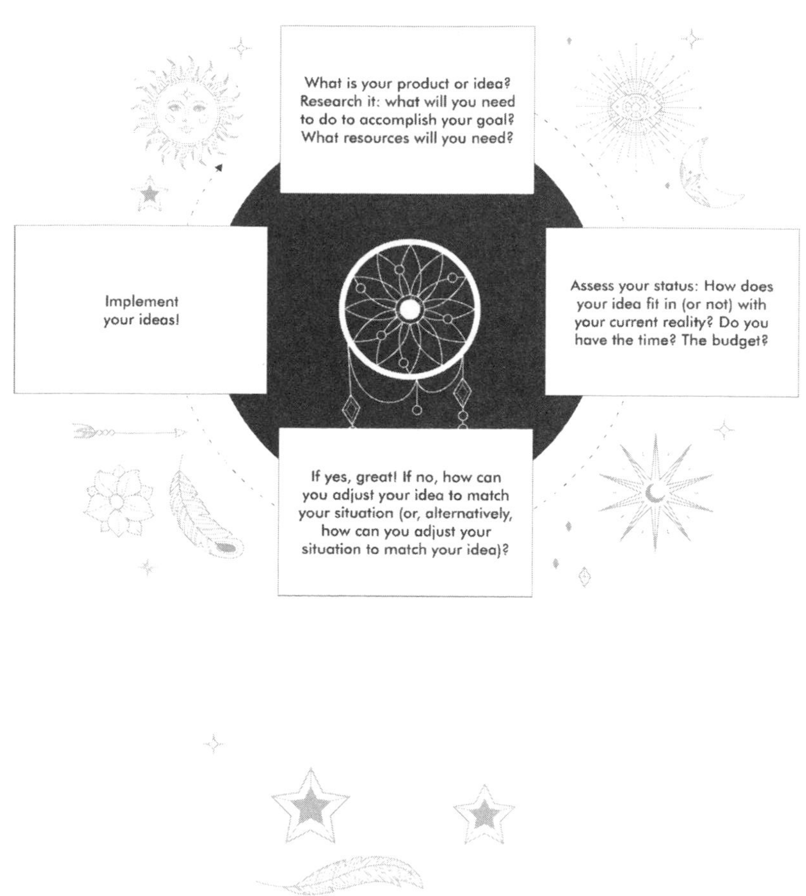

Step one, develop your idea. Research the ins and outs of the project, marketing initiative, partnership, whatever it is. What resources will you need? Budget, time, energy, people? Step two, assess your status. How do the stats of this idea line up with your current situation in time and space? What's your budget? What are your resources? And most importantly, do I give a fu@$? Step three, make adjustments as needed! If you lack the necessary resources, this step might mean developing your idea on a smaller scale to accommodate your budget, or seeing how you might go about increasing your budget to fit the needs of your idea. Step four, get to work. Hash out a plan and implement your idea. What's next? Rinse and repeat. Like many of our charts (and this book itself, actually!), this one is cyclical: when you develop an idea and see it to fruition, your work doesn't end. Another way to think of it: If you develop an idea and it doesn't pan out, you don't throw in the towel. You go back to square one. You research, and re-research, and re-re-research.

If you were hoping for clearer answers in this chapter, sorry to burst your bubble! We'd love to see you on WotB to discuss your options further, but when it comes down to it, channeling the Divine Feminine means taking responsibility for what's yours. That might sound like a masculine trait when taken at face value, but let's break that down. We don't mean you can't ask for guidance, and we don't mean "be controlling" or "don't compromise." We just mean "do your homework and soul-searching before committing to anything." The Divine Feminine is maternal and independent; she is creative and intuitive; she is wise and collected. Any decision she makes is hers and hers alone. This means a) don't let anyone derail you from your peace or encroach on your boundaries and leadership, and b) you are accountable for the choices you make. Discernment and mindfulness will always be "queen" in decision-making for your business and your life.

"I love the business development wheel because it is a cycle! Business is a constant flow of energy—constant change, if you want to grow. No matter what the initiative is, you can use this cycle. Recently I worked with Korie, and the idea was taking my products to retail. So step one was to research it thoroughly and we did—and things seemed to align. Then we went to step two. The issue was timing; I simply did not have the time to devote to a full retail launch. So off to step three: I still want to do retail, I just needed to create a better timeline and get some assets and staff in place for the effort. Step four: The implementation was a small test in small box retail and a plan for future big box. It seems simple, and I hope everyone reading this book will consciously use the wheel, but it's hard to put into practice. We want our ideas to come to fruition, now, and we tend to 'plow' instead of learning the art of discernment, which this wheel teaches."

Ashley Black

MOVEMENT #9: BUSINESS DEVELOPMENT WHEEL

We hope this chapter and our business development wheel got your gears turning. For this Movement, we'd like to keep the good times rolling and invite you to fill out your own business development wheel to reflect an idea you're interested in developing. We encourage you to be specific, here: Don't half-ass your research, and don't go too easy on yourself! Be realistic about your needs and about your resources, because if you aren't upfront with yourself from the get-go about what you can take on (or what you want to take on), you could wind up regretting it later.

This Movement is a two-parter: there's a "rinse and repeat" to this chart. So once you've filled out the chart to reflect all the research you've done, ask yourself, *What next?* If your idea worked, brava! Now, what else do you want to accomplish? How can you build on your initial idea? If your idea didn't work out the first time around, what new research can you do? What new questions can you ask yourself? Like a scientist, you are performing little research experiments to see what works for you and what doesn't. And when your research doesn't pan out, try, try again.

Round One:

BUSINESS DEVELOPMENT WHEEL

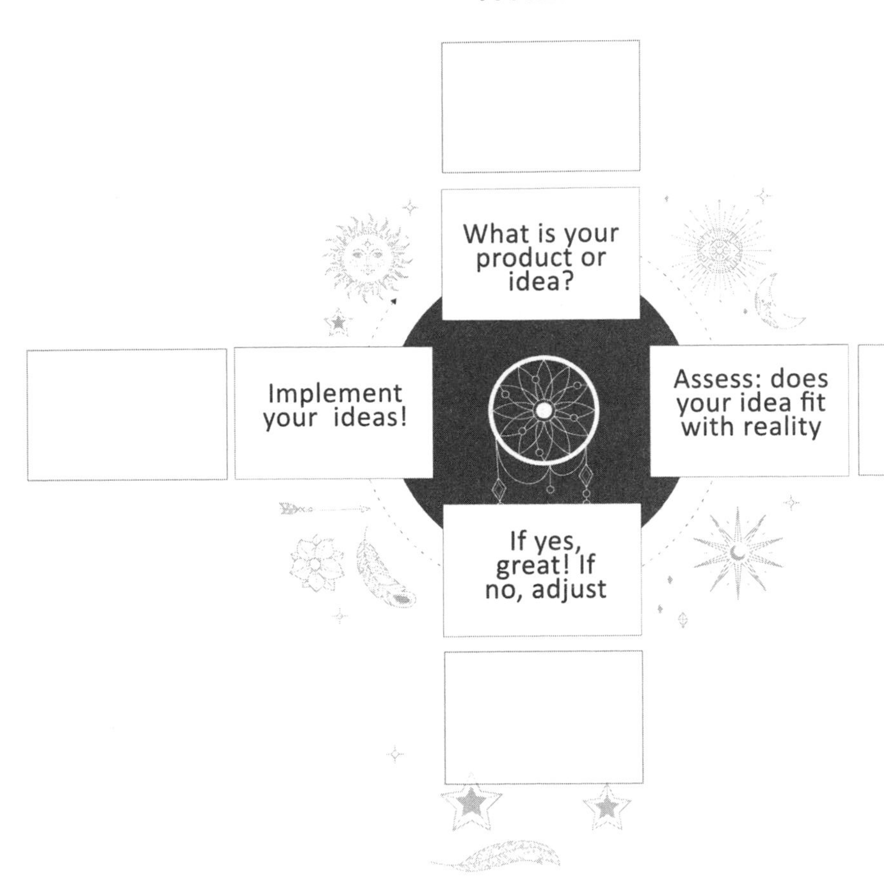

Rinse and Repeat:

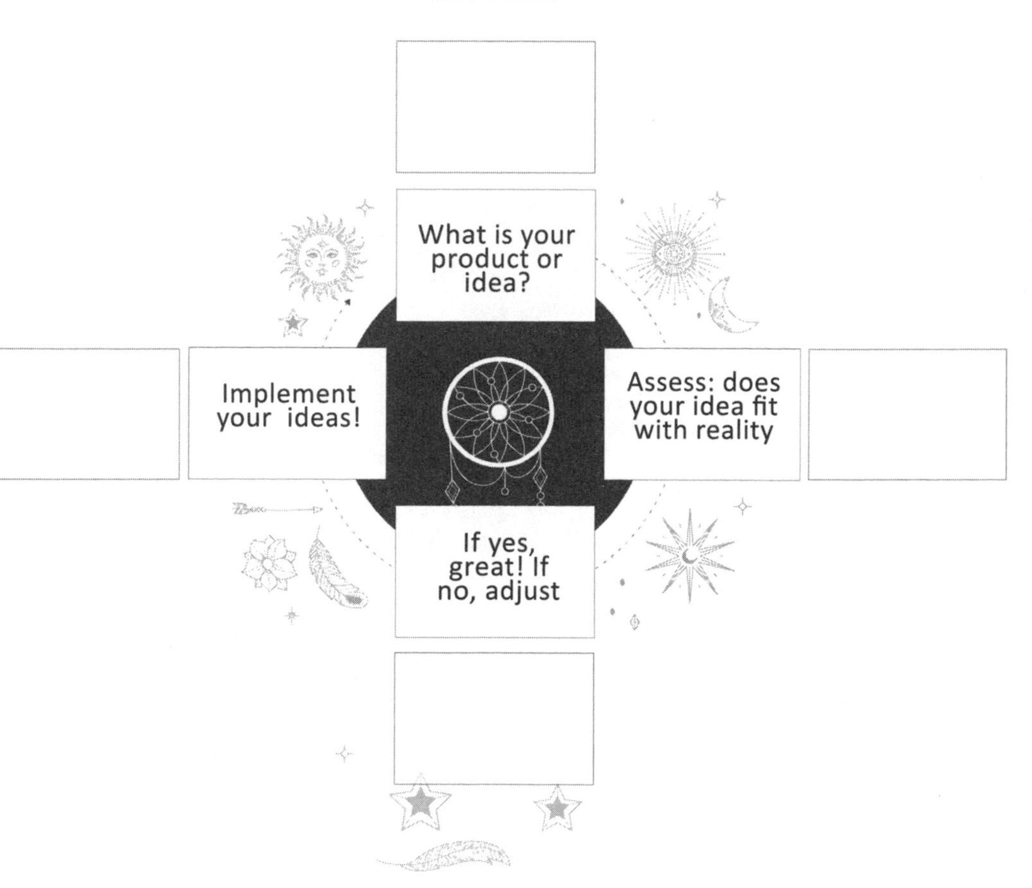

PART IV

Prosperity

❀ CHAPTER TEN ❀

BE...Clear

Sarah Eggenberger

Editor-at-Large, *NewBeauty*

Sarah Eggenberger is the editor-at-large for *NewBeauty* magazine. She's also beautiful, vivacious, and the mother of two children—sounds like she "has it all," doesn't it? Sarah would be the first to say that's not true! As Sarah says, "You can feel it in your heart... you have to compromise. There's no such thing as balance." Whether you're just starting out in your business or you're already thriving and trying to figure out what's next, being realistic about the shifts you must make to achieve your vision of prosperity sometimes means relinquishing your grip on the notion of "having it all." "So what are you gonna give up?" Sarah asks. "Is it a clean house? Is it exercise? Is it time with your friends? Is it sleep? Where can you carve out those times in your day...and what do you have to subtract? It's always a give-and-take. It's your life. You choose what works for you. You have to meditate and reflect." We love this attitude. Sarah might seem blunt about the struggle to "have it all," but by taking a realistic and direct approach to her dream life, she's able to prioritize her goals and cut out the BS. In the chapters to follow, we're going to piggyback off of Sarah's wisdom and guidance and walk YOU through the same process of clarifying your vision of prosperity—and then making it happen.

instagram.com/SarahEggenberger

HAVING IT ALL?
SHOOTING PAST THE FINISH LINE

You've probably seen runners compete in a race before, or maybe you've run a race yourself. You've likely noticed that when a runner is approaching the finish line, they don't consider the finish line the actual end point. Instead, they visualize the end point as some distance *beyond* the finish line; if they aim to stop running *at* the finish line, they will slow down as they approach and lose momentum. In a similar way, many entrepreneurs make the mistake of viewing the monetary success of their business venture as the finish line. But as we've said before—and we will say it again!—money is only a small piece of a full, passion-driven, purpose-fueled, prosperous life.

Money is not the finish line.

If you were to stop reading this book right now—if you were to achieve financial stability in your business and not spend a second thought on the idea of "prosperity"—you would be where many entrepreneurs find themselves: putting all their time and energy into their work. Some entrepreneurs don't slow down to consider what financial success is, or what success is in general. If you can't identify what success looks and feels like, then you can't intentionally manifest it.

So...what *is* success?

Like we said a few chapters ago, there's nothing wrong with having money. There's nothing wrong with being rich. But is being a millionaire or billionaire your finish line? What does it mean to "have it all," anyway? We want to encourage you to be like the runner and shoot PAST the finish line. In fact, we want to encourage you to never think of the finish line as being static, but something that continually changes location as you expand your vision for your life.

WHAT DOES HAPPY LOOK LIKE?

In his *Atlantic* article, "Your Professional Decline is Coming (Much) Sooner than You Think," happiness scholar Arthur C. Brooks tells a story of being on an overnight flight and overhearing the elderly man behind him confess to his wife that he wished he were dead. Brooks couldn't see what the man looked like, but, naturally, he imagined the death wish came from someone who had toiled throughout their life in obscurity, maybe somebody with regrets or a series of failures under the belt. But then Brooks writes, "At the end of the flight, as the lights switched on, I finally got a look at the desolate man. I was shocked. I recognized him—he was, and still is, world-famous. Then in his mid-80s, he was beloved as a hero for his courage, patriotism, and accomplishments many decades ago." The incident caused Brooks to wonder—how can somebody so successful, so celebrated, be so miserable? And would Brooks one day feel the same way? "Would I one day be looking back wistfully and wishing I were dead?" he writes. "Was there anything I could do, starting now, to give myself a shot at avoiding misery—and maybe even achieve happiness—when the music inevitably stops?"

This story isn't singular: it represents a sort of cognitive dissonance all too common in our society full of people who work hard for success and receive everything they *think* they want, only to discover it's not enough, or that it doesn't last forever. But the story also shows us that our society holds very specific ideas about who "should" be happy; Brooks assumed the man who spoke of wanting to die was unsuccessful in his life and was shocked to realize the man was a wealthy, celebrated hero. And we'll admit we were *also* shocked at that revelation. This is because the culturally accepted definition of "success" involves everything this man seems to be—and yet the man was miserable. So...what *does* happiness constitute?

As an entrepreneur and a woman, you've probably heard the term "having it all." The phrase was coined by the writer Helen Gurley Brown in her 1982 book *Having It All: Love, Success, Sex, and Money...Even If You're Starting with Nothing*, and it's become ubiquitous in the last few decades since then. The term is generally used to describe a woman who has managed to pull off a thriving professional *and* personal life: She has a husband and children and she has great relationships with all of them, and she *also* works hard at her high-paying career in her chosen field, in which she is a top girl boss who brings home the bacon. She has it all.

Or does she? As the writer Ruchi Saini points out in the *Times of India* article, "Having it all, redefined: Every woman gets to have her own definition. Don't let unrealistic expectations burden you":

> If "having it all" refers to a woman's happiness and well-being, then why can't a single woman, a single mother, a childfree woman, or a homemaker be seen as having it all? [...] [T]here is no single definition of happiness and success, and they mean different things for different people. The reductive notion that only

> women who have both a career and a family can be considered as successful and/or happy ignores the complexity of human personalities and desires.

Saini goes on to point out that the notion of "having it all" (which, mind you, is *exclusively* used to describe women's aspirations, and never men's) is incredibly heteronormative:

> [I]f you are a married woman with a career, then "having it all" becomes a patriarchal shorthand for "doing it all," especially if you have limited access to childcare or are still climbing the professional ladder. [...] There is no glory in drudgery, and that is exactly what "having it all" encompasses for a regular, middle-class woman who wishes to climb the professional ladder while managing a family.

So what *does* it mean to "have it all"? We encourage you, reader, to ask that question of yourself, and to avoid taking for granted the ideas of "prosperity" taken from society's samskaras and ingrained at an early age. It's grown-ass women time, and you get to stand up here for what YOU want. You don't have to take on anyone else's definition of prosperity; you get to define it for yourself.

And when you're asked what you want, we invite you to ask yourself why, and don't just say, "Because it will make me happy." Why will it make you happy? Go beyond your impulse answers and study what essential need or needs that answer will satisfy. For instance, instead of saying, "I want to make a million dollars a year," ask yourself what would that million dollars pay for? Is it for a dream house that is filled with spaces you love, a connection with nature, a home office to eliminate a commute to work? Or is it the (perceived) prestige that comes with a status-symbol house?

If you say, "I want to own my own restaurant"—why? When you visualize the day-in and day-out grind, does that excite you? Consider the potential reality: Will it make you sad that you might not be home at nights to be with family or have time to cultivate a romantic relationship? What about THAT?

Maybe you say, "I want kids and the love of my life," but do you? Or are you really picturing yourself having cocktails with friends in your Louboutins, talking about closing your deals? (Or vice versa!) No matter what you want, just make sure it's what YOU want. The REAL YOU. Free of limiting beliefs, free of samskara habits, free of "the dream of the planet." Prosperity is about you! Y.O.U. Your authentic desires that are uniquely yours!

It seems like it should be so easy to know what you want, and yet, when we're put on the spot, we often have no clue. We typically theoretically know what we want, and we say vague things like "I want to be happy," or "I just want to be financially secure" but we can't answer *detailed* questions about what that looks like. And that's an issue, because this book isn't just about thinking about what you want, it's about helping you actually manifest it. Remember Natasha's 5 Pillars of Manifestation from chapter two. She points out that before you can achieve prosperity, you need clarity of vision. Well, that's what this chapter is all about: getting clear.

"For me, I grew up with a mother that instilled happiness on the daily. She was hyper-clear and reminded us of our brilliance, our beautiful innate ability to create impact in the world, and our human mission to share warmth. She etched pillars of confidence, strength, fulfillment, and a desire to fight for our truth. My father was also an amazing contributor of intellectual pursuit who guided us to challenge the status quo, teaching us to form a goal-oriented approach and the skills to be a master problem-solver. My journey has always led to a clear path of diverse friends, extreme loyalty, faith in other people. I believe that every individual on earth and entrepreneurial journey can be filled with great access to achievement. For me the greatest joy has come in the form of profound friendships with my mentors, bosses, business associates, clients, partners, community, family, friends, and strangers. Happiness for me is leaving a legacy of laughter, love, and an enriched zest for all things. Clarity for me is sharing the journey with others, teaching them what I know, and learning from them what they know."

K

Korie Minkus

Societal roles—especially gender roles—are a huge factor in what we believe we want or say we want. When our divine gender energies are out of alignment, we are susceptible to societal pressure to perform specific roles and to do so gladly.

But when we check in with our authentic selves, and when our Divine Masculine and Feminine energies are in balance with one another, what does our *want* look like? What is our true heart's desire? What if our future was a blank canvas? What paints are you choosing and what are you going to create? And what is your WHY?

It's not easy to simply defy the pressure of our hypermasculine, consumerist society. It's not easy to play by your own rules. But here's a fun fact: While studies indicate that female entrepreneurs are much unhappier than their male counterparts when they first go into business—we know, you're freaking out at that bit of info right now, but wait, it gets better! According to the *Forbes* article "Female Entrepreneurs Are Happier Than Male Entrepreneurs," those *same* studies also analyzed the happiness levels of entrepreneurs who were further into their careers, and the results indicated that established female entrepreneurs are actually much *happier* than their male counterparts. Now, we feel for the men—of course we do. But these studies may indicate that while there are way more initial barriers for women in the workplace to overcome than men, once those women get through the door and get their business underway, the Divine Feminine qualities that initially may have made entering the entrepreneurial world a challenge actually serve them in the long run—qualities like following your heart, embracing your intuition, and valuing love and connection over competition and workaholism—qualities our culture doesn't generally associate with professional success. Embracing your authentic, Divine Feminine self can help you thrive.

"For me, I had to 'have it all' before I realized that I needed to architect my life better. I was a millionaire, living between my LA and Houston mansions, with amazing kids, a successful business, the designer clothes, the Aston Martin, the Cartier, and travel galore. The private jets, the yachts, the celebrity friends. I had more money than I could spend, but I spent all my time making more. I had lost my connection to nature, I had a hard time being present because I was stressed all the time, my self-care was in the toilet, and I wasn't truly open for a love relationship. When I came up for air and got real about what I really wanted, I realized I had created someone else's fantasy life. So I did a 180. I moved to a place of more healthy, like-minded individuals who lived a more simple life. I now only work from 10:00 a.m. to 2:00 p.m. each day. I spend mornings on self-care, introspection, and growth. My life is completely full and my vision crystal-clear. I could have kept going full steam and I would probably be 'way more successful' if I did, but I'm glad I didn't. For the first time, I gave myself permission to examine what I truly wanted. Turns out, I'm a simple bitch. And I'm getting more simple by the minute! LOL."

Ashley Black

All this talk of your heart's desire and what it means to be happy maybe sounds a little sappy. But the thing is, it only sounds sappy because we're used to putting up the cold, invulnerable exterior that the world tells us we need in order to thrive. In our patriarchal society, being a girl boss usually means "having it all," and "having it all" usually means achieving everything a woman is "supposed" to want: kids, husband, job, white picket fence. There's not much room leftover for dreams beyond that. We've been handed a prescription for happiness and success and we keep swallowing the pills, until we don't. We're here to help you throw away that prescription and give you unbridled permission to completely revamp your vision for your life, right here and right now.

So like Sarah Eggenberger advises, let's be decisive about what we want. Let's design a life, and then we can see where your business fits in. We encourage you to strip away any preconceived notions and just give yourself permission to be YOU. Don't think about society or your job or your husband or your kids or where you need to live or what your parents need at this point—we will fit that all in. And don't think about HOW you're going to attain this. This is about creating a dream life. Your dream life. With no judgment or attachment to the process whatsoever. To help you do this, we've created a powerful Movement called the 6 Bowls. By engaging in this exercise, it is our hope that you will begin to clarify what your vision is for your daily life before taking any action toward achieving that life. If you can get clarity on where to direct your time and attention, the energy will certainly flow.

"For me, happiness is a life filled with activities that feed my soul. Yes, I'm fulfilled by the many different hats I wear, whether it's producing, creating events, building brands, strategizing, workshopping. I'm very engaged in the professional life I'm living. I'm exhilarated by in-depth brainstorming sessions with my clients, and I love conceptualizing and executing a compelling video out of nothing but a few ideas jotted down on a piece of paper. While I've found success in the world of visuals, in my heart I feel most fulfilled when I see someone have a positive breakthrough about who they are and everything that's possible for them. I'm my truest self when I'm holding space for someone to shine. Buddha said it best: 'Thousands of candles can be lit from a single candle and the life of the candle will not be shortened. Happiness never decreases from being shared.'"

L

Lisa Vrancken

MOVEMENT #10: 6 BOWLS OF HIGH-VIBRATIONAL LIVING

The goal of the 6 Bowls Movement is to help you examine the gaps between your ideal future and your present reality and see where you can rechannel energy to live more purposefully and more passionately. Where would you like to focus your attention? It may not seem like that big of a deal to spend most of your day in Time to Make the Donuts mode, but, as author Annie Dillard wrote, "How we spend our days is, of course, how we spend our lives. What we do with this hour, and that one, is what we are doing." How do you want to spend your hour? Your day? Your life?

In order to perform the 6 Bowls Movement, you will need a few things:

- Six bowls (surprise, surprise!).
- A camera.
- Thirty-two small objects. These can be marbles, buttons, paperclips, pennies, even Cheerios or gumballs—whatever you have on hand.

The thirty-two small objects you've collected represent two days' worth of waking hours (this is assuming you get roughly eight hours of sleep a night), and the six bowls you'll be putting them in represent six major areas of a high-vibrational Life—**Inner Light**, **Outer Light**, **Whole-istic**, **Social Time**, **Bread-and-Butter**, and **Passion Project**. Before we begin this Movement, let's spend a minute going over these terms....

Inner Light is the starting point of personal growth. This bowl represents time spent on activities that feed your soul and expand your mind. Activities that nourish inner light include attending a great yoga class, reading a good book, or walking in nature. Inner Light practices cultivate brain states that alleviate anxiety, jump-start energy, and stimulate creativity. The ultimate Inner Light activity is meditation. Inner Light activities are just for us and done alone. It's shining all the energy we have inward to our heart. Some can even achieve high gamma brain waves when performing Inner Light activities, and Inner Light work is essential for life and brain balance.

If Inner Light is self-care and introspection, **Outer Light** is care for the world around you. This bowl represents time spent on activities that positively impact others and our planet. Just like Inner Light, Outer Light looks different for everyone; you might shine your Outer Light by donating to your local food bank, mentoring others, or working in your community garden—or maybe you focus your Outer Light on your household by spending time with your children. It might take some careful consideration to know how you shine your Outer Light, and that's OK! Think of Outer Light as sharing your special gifts, a very high-vibrational activity.

The **Whole-istic** bowl represents the ways in which you take care of your physical vessel for this human experience—your body. As we learned in earlier chapters and the high-vibrational foods chart, taking in sunlight and eating those phytonutrients are wonderful Whole-istic activities. Getting massages (or FasciaBlasting), taking a long walk, or getting a gym sesh in can all be part of the Whole-istic bowl. Sisters, we only get one body in which to experience this life, and we know that it has a frequency, and we need that frequency to resonate with the things we want to attract. Far too often, we hear, "I need to take better care of myself." Taking care of the physical body is a precursor to honing your passion and fulfilling your purpose. You might notice there's some overlap between Whole-istic and Inner Light; that's because, as it turns out, personal growth is difficult without attending to your basic needs!

Social Time is...well...time spent socializing! In his book *The Blue Zones of Happiness*, *National Geographic* journalist Dan Buettner identifies the happiest people as those who spend three to six hours a day socializing. What the #%^&? Six hours? I know what you're thinking: *Who has time to socialize at all, let alone for three to six hours a day?!* But consider that socializing isn't always going out for a wild night on the town with a party of gal pals. Socializing is also devoting quality time to your partner, family time, catching up with coworkers at the water cooler, or even chatting with the barista who makes your latte every morning, if it's done mindfully. Psychologist Susan Pinker identifies "weak bonds" (your relationship with your barista, your postman, the woman you see walking her dog at the same time as you every morning) as just as important to a healthy life as "strong bonds" (your relationship with your family and close friends). For this exercise, we just want you to know that happiness is what you desire; then, statistically speaking, you gotta put some energy here.

Bread-and-Butter is what you do for money. It would be great if your Passion Project and your Bread-and-Butter business were one and the same, and for some people they are.

But for many people, that isn't the case (or not yet, anyway!). Bread-and-Butter might not only involve the time you literally spend working; it might also include all the tasks necessary to facilitate your work, such as preparing lunches, commuting, hiring childcare, attending conferences, and more. Your Bread-and-Butter is what you do to make money and make sure life is handled. A large majority of people spend their entire day in survival mode and all the good juju goes to Bread-and-Butter. For this exercise we want to bring awareness to the amount of time you actually *want* to spend on your Bread-and-Butter.

In the same way, when we talk about your **Passion Project**, we are focused not only on the literal hours involved in your passion project, whatever state it's in—whether fledgling hobby, full-on side-hustle, or your full-time work. This book is about passion, so obviously we want you to direct some energy here to honor your soul's desire. This could be strategizing the business plan, getting involved in a specific project for your favorite charity, going back to school, or taking classes or retreats. It's the thing(s) you would probably LOVE to spend a lot of time doing.

Now let's begin!

Step 1: Label the Bowls

Start by labeling each of your six bowls with one of the above terms—Inner Light, Outer Light, Whole-istic, Social Time, Bread-and-Butter, and Passion Project.

Step 2: Design Your Dream Life

Imagine that you have **unlimited time and money.** You have total freedom to create the life you want to live and direct the energy of your day exactly where you want to. This Movement calls on you to channel your Divine Feminine energy—to rely on your intuition and inner peace. Have faith the universe will provide for your every need, as long as you live authentically. What does living authentically look like?

Think about this for a few moments, considering which bowls would receive the most time and attention: would your Outer Light bowl receive most of your attention? Maybe your Bread-and-Butter bowl will receive hardly any attention at all! Maybe you want to become a monk and spend most of your time in Inner Light. Maybe you're ready to rock out a large portion of the day in your Passion Project or maybe you crave more time with family. There are no wrong "wants!" This is your chance to design how you spend your day. So, when you are ready, gather your small objects—one for two full days' worth of conscious hours. Divide your thirty-two hours between the six bowls, according to how much time and energy you would give each bowl if you had complete and total control over your time and money. If you've noticed, we didn't include low-vibrational bowls such as scrolling through Instagram or arguing with your spouse, with the assumption that you would want a high-vibrational life. (Of course you do!)

Once you've arranged your small objects in their appropriate "I want" bowls, take a minute to reflect on the blueprint you've created; does this energy distribution feel right? Can you visualize what this plan might look like in action? Do you feel happy, joyful, and fulfilled imagining yourself living this life? Most importantly, does it bring you peace and enlightenment, the two highest vibrational emotions? Keep rearranging your bowls as needed, until you feel totally at ease with the two days of dream life you've conjured up.

When you feel satisfied with your dream life, take a photo of the bowls.

Step 3: Describe Your Current Reality

Ready to set an intention in motion? Empty the bowls of their contents, and this time around, we'll be looking at your life as it actually is. Then we will work at closing the gap through transference of energy.

Think about your day-to-day. Where does your attention go? Maybe your bowls are evenly split; maybe you don't spend enough energy on living Wholeistically, or you spend too much time on Outer Light stuff. Keep it real, now. No BS—living authentically requires you to be authentic about your life, including the imperfections! This is the time to really be raw. There is no judgment in just calling a spade a spade. Think over a typical week and organize the objects where you place your focus. Keep in mind that many people are rushing in a river of "make it happen" and have a lack of mindfulness around designing their dream life. So, whether your reality bowls are miles away from your dream life, or quite close, it doesn't matter for this part of the Movement, this is an "it is what it is" exercise.

When you have arranged your bowls to reflect your daily reality, take a photo of the bowls. Revisit it as many times as it takes to get it accurate.

Step 4: Compare the Bowls

Observe the photos of your dream life and your current reality side by side. How well do they match up? The goal is for there to be no difference, but if your bowls are severely mismatched, don't feel discouraged! The first step to living your dream life is becoming aware of where you need to redirect. You can consider one small alteration, or you can plan an overhaul. The main thing is to start taking steps today to start living your life in vibratory alignment with your ideal future. How can you begin to close the gap between your dreams and your reality?

The purpose of the 6 Bowls Movement is not to do it once and never look back, but to perform it regularly to reflect your life as it transforms, because expansion isn't instantaneous; it can happen in micro-movements that become monumental! Simply put, each time you perform the 6 Bowls Movement, the difference between your current reality and your dream life should shrink. You can always pivot to make the tweaks necessary to start living your dream life. It's never too late. It's as simple as taking energy from one bowl and directing it into a new bowl. You can be like Ashley and go balls to the walls, or you can move one tiny object at a time and allow that change to settle in. The whole idea is to do SOMETHING! Lean into living your dream life here, make a shift, and be open for the universe to provide the path. They say *an object in motion stays in motion*, so let's move some energy, sisters!

❀ CHAPTER ELEVEN ❀

BE...Visionary

Kim Russo

The Happy Medium
Author, Medium

Remember Nikola Tesla's words, from chapter two? "If you want to find the secrets of the universe, think in terms of energy, frequency and vibration." It's a perfect mantra for this book, right? Well, it's even more relevant to Kim Russo's calling as the Happy Medium: "The other side is vibrating at a quicker frequency than we are here in the dense third dimension.... Me being the medium, I am the antenna that picks up on the signals from the higher frequencies." We were so excited to sit down with Kim in the WotB and get the inside scoop on how she picks up on frequencies from other dimensions—and how *we* can become more aware of our energy in *this* dimension. Kim encourages us to step out of the pressure of the collective consciousness, which she says has many of us non-mediums falling asleep to our power and our purpose; by becoming aware, by *visualizing* our power to live our most authentic, high-vibrational lives, we are able to meet our potential. There is an opportunity here, ladies, for you to not only architect that beautiful life you designed in the 6 Bowls Movement, but to *make it happen.* And nobody can make it happen but YOU! "Everyone has to authentically stay in their own space and do their own work,

and if they do not, the universe is going to pull the rug," Kim says. "You have to ask yourself, 'Who am I fooling? Am I just putting things off that my higher self says I should be doing but I'm ignoring?' You can't ignore it anymore, because then the universe is going to make it happen the way it should, but not necessarily in the way you would have liked it to happen." Trust the universe, ladies! It'll do its thing, even if you don't believe it will. So don't sit idly by while life happens to you. Take CONTROL of your future!

facebook.com/kimthehappymedium
instagram.com/kimrussomedium
twitter.com/thehappymedium
youtube.com/user/TheHappymediumkim

MANIFEST IT!

Sometimes, it can be simple to point to a lifelong goal, like starting your own business, and say, "That's my dream!" But it can be a little overwhelming to actualize that dream in practice. (And, like Kim Russo says, it can be tempting to just ignore the hints your higher self gives you and keep on sleeping through life!) In this chapter, we are going to set these dreams in motion, give them intention, and manifest the hell out of them. Wake up, bitches, it's time to take your dream life and make it a reality.

Arthur C. Brooks and other scholars of the psychology of happiness attest: When you concretize your goals, you are more likely to achieve them. The law of attraction is real, babes! You gotta know what you want and have the faith that it'll happen before you can make it happen. Manifestation works. Research indicates athletes achieve greater success in their sport when they first visualize their performance. In fact, science shows that our brain doesn't know the difference between visualizing something and it actually happening. Manifestation works in just the same way: by believing it is possible, it becomes possible. We know, we know, we just said dreaming alone isn't going to get you anywhere, and we mean that. When we say it "becomes possible," we don't mean it just happens magically. It becomes possible because manifestation gives you the strength to believe you can achieve what some might consider unachievable goals. And achieving those goals starts with awareness. You can't expand your life until you become aware of what you need to expand.

In the last Movement, you constructed your ideal life and you compared it to your present reality. For this chapter's Movement, we're going to help you put your dream life into action by creating a **vision board**. A vision board is a visual representation of your dream life, designed by you, created with the purpose of helping you become more intentional about achieving that life. It's time to manifest your future, ladies. To help you prepare for the vision board Movement, we'd like to share the divine numbers 3-6-9 discussed by Nikola Tesla. We have incorporated the numbers 3-6-9 into a Manifestation Method. The 3-6-9 method asks that you create three manifestation statements, write them down, and look at each of them six times a day for nine seconds each. Your statements should be centered on a high-vibrational feeling (such as gratitude, happiness, or peace) and something you want to manifest—but root your statements in the present, because, like Kim Russo says, "There's no more time 'tomorrow,' don't say, 'I'll do it tomorrow.' Everything has to happen right now because we're creating the future right now." The time is now!

Try following this format:

> *I am* [high-vibrational feeling] *because of* [thing you want to manifest] *because* [the reason what you manifest makes you feel the way it does].
>
> For example:
>
> I am grateful for my beautiful, healthy body because it makes me feel strong and sexy.
>
> or
>
> I am thankful for and exhilarated by my new house on the river because it makes me feel free and connected.
>
> or
>
> I am grateful for and elated by my first million-dollar year in business because it makes me feel proud and motivated.

Hopefully you get the idea. It's all about framing your dream life around gratitude.

Take a second to think about three manifestation statements you could design to incorporate into your daily 3-6-9 practice, and then write them in the chart below. You can use the chart as a guide to form the manifestation sentences and then save this for your vision board.

Manifestation statements

	High-vibrational feeling	Because of/for	Thing you want to manifest		Why does it make you feel this way?
I am				because	
I am				because	
I am				because	

This mini-Movement is rooted in *I am, I am, I am*. As Dr. Ona Brown says, "Start with the *I am*, with the two most powerful words in the English language. I am love. I am light. I am peace. I am joy. I am worthy." Beginning your day with manifestation statements is such a powerful way to tame your neural pathways to achieve your dreams.

We in the BE... community swear by the 3-6-9 Movement and hope you'll consider incorporating it into your daily practice (and sharing your manifestation statements with the ladies in the WotB so we can cheer you on!). But stick around: in the Movement to follow, we'll show you how to apply your manifestation statements to a vision board to give you even more clarity of purpose. There is great power in intention, particularly when the intention is founded in gratitude and other high-vibrational feelings. **Trust! This! Process!** What you put into the universe will find its way back to you, especially if you don't attempt to control the process, and take action where you can towards the things you want.

MOVEMENT #11: VISION BOARD

When we were writing this book and tossing ideas around, we were astounded at how many people had never created a vision board or weren't currently using one. Like, WHAT THE $%^&?! A vision board is one of the most powerful tools you can use. In fact, most people who concentrate their vision boards on long-term goals find they end up accomplishing those goals in a much shorter time period. That's because... well...this shit works. You can find scores of articles on the internet about the power of the vision board and how you can make your own, and renowned thinkers like Oprah Winfrey and Deepak Chopra have sung the vision board's praises. Needless to say, vision boards are incredibly popular.

Like we said, a vision board is a visual representation of your dream life, architected with the purpose of helping you become more intentional about reaching your goals. Since your brain doesn't know the difference between visualization and actualization, when you look at your vision board, you are not just imagining what you see, you are EXPERIENCING it and raising your vibration to attract the elements of it. The visualization process can change your physical chemicals and neurotransmitters, changing your electromagnetic field. You are literally emitting vibes like a tuning fork, searching for the frequencies of your goals. We encourage you to make your vision board special. Use fun supplies. Make it beautiful. We also want to encourage you to make it digital as well, or travel size. You can cut and paste right into a word doc. You could make it on poster board and take a picture of it and have it printed. And one more thing—we're doing our vision boards with a twist: We're going to use the manifestation statements you just created for the 3-6-9 method as a jumping-off point to give your vision board that much more precision and intentionality.

So get ready, ladies. We're going to help your dreams come true.

"As part of my New Year, New You program I do every year, I lead millions of followers in making vision boards. For mine, I had about three to five years in mind. Well, after about six months I had achieved everything on the vision board and then some, and the things I didn't achieve, I learned I didn't want anymore. I just recently made another one, with my partner Jordi (he is a big vision-board guy, which I find super sexy!). We made separate boards, but we did it together, collecting pictures and sharing ours with each other. It was actually difficult because we are extremely content in the life we've already manifested. But that is a signal that it is time to expand. We started putting things like perfect bodies, surf moves above our skill level, places we wanted to travel, and private planes on our boards. Your vision board is not only to help you manifest quickly, it's to help you manifest exponentially until you're living a life beyond what you could never have dreamed of."

A

Ashley Black

INSTRUCTIONS

- Take the three statements you made in the 3-6-9 method. These will be the manifestation statements you base your vision board around! Gather images and text related to your vision for the future, and something to create your masterpiece on—as long as it's something that you can see every day, six times a day. It's really easy, once you have clarity about *what* you want. Use Google Images and search things like "healthy body," "house in Italy," "money imagery," etc. Try to find images that evoke your emotions.

  There's really no "right" way to make a vision board, so long as your final product reveals a vision of your goals for the future that you can see every day. Whatever gets you jazzed up to look at. You can even get a little crafty: get a photo album ready to draw from, grab some markers, maybe some stamps or stencils, old magazines, maybe some feathers or rhinestones or glitter—who knows?! The possibilities are endless!

- Life coach Zakiya Larry suggests considering whether your vision board should be short-term or long-term focused: Do you want to accomplish your manifestation statements this month? Or do you want to make a board to represent your one-, two- or five-year plan? In the article "Here's How to Make a Vision Board for Manifestation" published by Oprah Daily, Larry suggests somewhere in the middle, usually: She says making a vision board for the year is a great amount of time to focus on.

- Write or paste your 3 **manifestation statements** to your vision board—and you're off! You've got your vision, you've got all your artsy-fartsy materials, now it's time to lean into a creative alpha flow and follow your heart! Collage wherever the Divine Feminine takes you!

- When you're finished, put your vision board somewhere where you will see it often: hang it on the wall by your bed so it's the first thing you see in the morning, or if it's digital, make it your desktop background. Maybe you'll display it in your office or living room, so that you can talk to colleagues or friends about your goals. An article published by CNBC titled "How to stay committed to your goals" indicates that sharing your goals, especially with people you admire, is an incredibly helpful motivator, because it keeps you accountable. Ashley makes hers on an 11x14 piece of paper that is folded in her daily notebook. [<insert Icon_WotB_2.pdf>:We also encourage you to post your vision board in our social media so you can share your goals with other *BE*-ers! Make sure to use the hashtag #Mydreamlife. It's like having a gym partner—you've just committed to manifesting your dreams!]

- Like many of the Movements in this book, this isn't a one-and-doner: Vision boards are designed to be outgrown. When you've accomplished the goals on your vision board—or if those goals ever shift—make a new one. The future is always in motion, but if you can see it, you can achieve it.

"I've put the word 'mentor' on my board to remind myself of a role in my life that makes me feel whole. I've always wanted to write a book, and on one of my vision boards, I had cut out '#1 bestselling author' from a magazine. I believe I manifested my perfect co-authors, and the book in your hand is tangible proof that manifestation works. I'm a true Sagittarian and I love to travel. Seeing the world and experiencing different cultures has been a huge part of who I am, and I always put the next destination I'm attracted to on my board. And this time, I'm not looking to fly solo! I'm manifesting my twin flame, and I'm going for it all. No settling, ladies! While filling your vision board with gorgeous representations of your ambition is important, it's also important to include photos of the environments you feel your best in. In Japanese culture, a nature therapy called Shinrin-Yoku (or 'forest bathing') has been proven to dramatically raise physical, spiritual, and emotional health." (cont.)

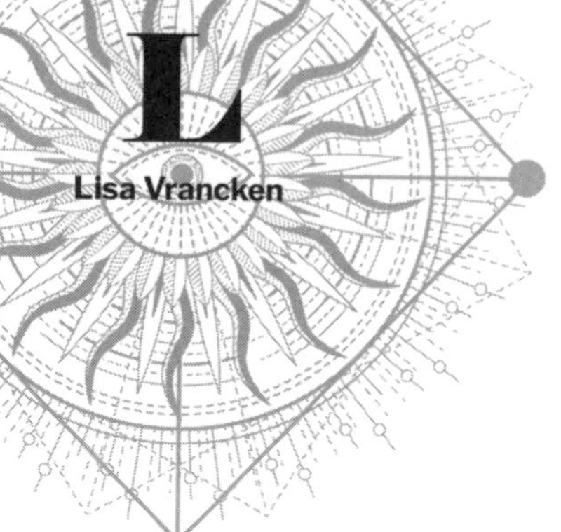

"When we feel drawn to move in a new direction, it's often our passion beckoning us toward a greater version of our life. Your intuition is a gift, an innate ability to understand without conscious reasoning. It requires self-reflection to uncover what lights your soul and makes your heart sing. Balancing your brain waves is a step toward alignment. When you unveil it, you can confidently share your beautiful gifts with the world. I believe this reveal requires a heart-centered approach. It starts with listening to yourself, getting to know yourself, and being present with you."

❀ CHAPTER TWELVE ❀

BE...Prosperous

Christa Orecchio

In this final chapter, we'd like to introduce you to Christa Orecchio, the founder and CEO of The Whole Journey. Christa is a clinical nutritionist, holistic health counselor, and single mom who learned how to strike a work-life balance in all aspects of health, time, money, and energy. She boldly chose to make a mid-career pivot and persevered in the face of seemingly insurmountable obstacles, according to her own personal idea of prosperity and wholeness. She did the work, made wise decisions with her time, and took calculated financial risks to shift her business in a new direction. "As a clinical nutritionist and holistic health counselor, my mission has always been to help people heal their bodies from the root cause, using food as medicine. This was my passion when I founded my private practice in 2005, but after eight years as a service provider I decided it was time to walk away. Why would I give up a thriving referral-only practice with a six-month waitlist? Because I realized that in all the growing and building, I was spending more and more of my time hiring and training clinical nutritionists and food specialists and less and less doing what I love: helping people. So, in 2013, I stepped away from my practice and pivoted to an online program." Through a fierce commitment, Christa revised her patterning, defined success on her own terms,

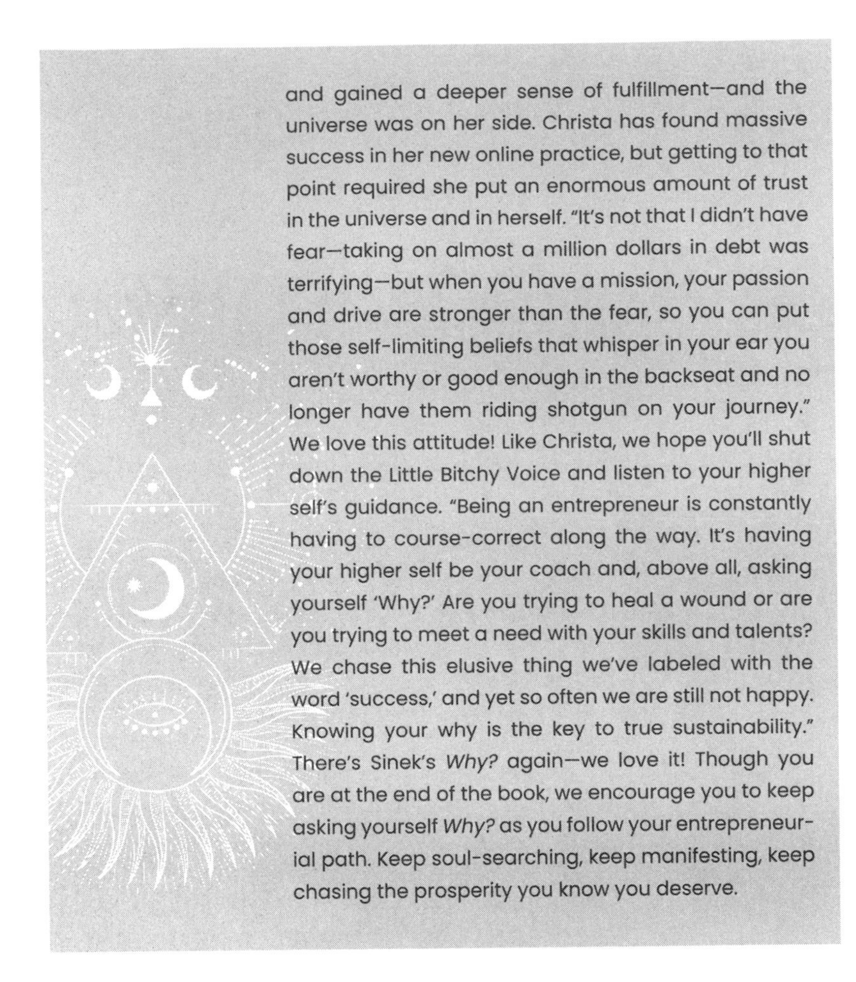

and gained a deeper sense of fulfillment—and the universe was on her side. Christa has found massive success in her new online practice, but getting to that point required she put an enormous amount of trust in the universe and in herself. "It's not that I didn't have fear—taking on almost a million dollars in debt was terrifying—but when you have a mission, your passion and drive are stronger than the fear, so you can put those self-limiting beliefs that whisper in your ear you aren't worthy or good enough in the backseat and no longer have them riding shotgun on your journey." We love this attitude! Like Christa, we hope you'll shut down the Little Bitchy Voice and listen to your higher self's guidance. "Being an entrepreneur is constantly having to course-correct along the way. It's having your higher self be your coach and, above all, asking yourself 'Why?' Are you trying to heal a wound or are you trying to meet a need with your skills and talents? We chase this elusive thing we've labeled with the word 'success,' and yet so often we are still not happy. Knowing your why is the key to true sustainability." There's Sinek's *Why?* again—we love it! Though you are at the end of the book, we encourage you to keep asking yourself *Why?* as you follow your entrepreneurial path. Keep soul-searching, keep manifesting, keep chasing the prosperity you know you deserve.

https://www.facebook.com/thewholejourney
https://www.instagram.com/thewholejourney
https://www.pinterest.com/thewholejourney
https://www.youtube.com/user/thewholejourney

THE END?

Well ladies, we have MADE IT. Twelve chapters, four parts, one book. Passion, Purpose, Product, Prosperity. We've talked about a lot in this slim volume, and we feel so honored that you've come along for the ride. We're going to take this final chapter to talk about something important, something our ultra-capitalist patriarchal society simply doesn't talk about enough: gratitude.

You can make your to-do lists. You can mark your calendars. You can create your vision boards and design your plans, you can arrange your six bowls, you can say your prayers and manifest your future. You can achieve your wildest dreams. But in the end, taking the time to be grateful and intentional (remember that word??) in your day-to-day life is an integral ingredient to a fulfilling existence.

So in the midst of this life of planning and budgeting and personal branding and endless work-life balancing...how do we manage to stay humble? How do we manage to not overshoot the goal, and create unintentional chaos or busyness with our success?

Whether you're just starting out on your entrepreneurial journey or you're making five, six, seven, eight, nine figures and wondering what's next for you and your business, we hope this book will be helpful for you to cycle through again and again, as your career shifts, as your goals shift, as you grow more and more into your authentic self. If we have learned anything in our time as entrepreneurs, it's that life is constantly in flux, and certain reminders for how to live a good life are evergreen—in fact, if you were to ask us how much of this book we invented, the answer is "very little." Everything you have read here, from the secrets to high-vibrational living to engaging with the Divine Feminine to managing your brain waves, is drawn from ancient teachings and modern-day interpretations. Every nugget of wisdom we have to offer is a nugget we have picked up on our own journeys and we hope that presenting it in this simple way will be game-changing for you.

"Growing up in a big family, playing team sports throughout my school years, and working in corporate, I learned repeatedly how ego can make or break a team. Ego can be a great source of strength. And it can be your greatest weakness if you allow ego to fill gaps of self-worth. What I discovered most is that ego evolves, and it can become a dominant default if we do not learn to let go of ego when it's not serving us. Fearful and unsure, I discovered the power in letting go of ego, to allow space to receive, listen, follow, accept, and honor. Separating ego from self-confidence, today I am grateful for the prosperity achieved and stand ready for the next untapped opportunity to be unstoppable."

K

Korie Minkus

So this final Movement is one that we hope will attest to the universality and timelessness of the advice proffered in these hundred-plus pages (which is also the advice we follow in our own lives). And it might seem like a surprising way to end this book.

It's time for an ego check.

What? Yes, an ego check! If there's one thing it's easy to forget as we grow in our power, it's humility and simplicity. It can be so easy to get wrapped up in the whirlwind of success and to place your ability to achieve above other important aspects of your life or of yourself, including family, friends, other dreams you may have, and the world at large. Staying humble goes hand in hand with assessing prosperity; it involves checking in with yourself *on the daily* to make sure you're staying grounded and aligned with the Divine Feminine and your authentic self.

"For me, I didn't realize that my ego was fueling my prosperity model in the beginning. I genuinely wanted to change the world. When doing my prosperity work, however, I was attached to the societal model of prosperity, with multiple houses, a super busy schedule, the real jet setter lifestyle—until I achieved it. With that level of success came a lot of unwanted attention and complications that aren't aligned with TRUE Ashley. I did conscious work around quieting the ego—such as taking trips to India, imbibing Ayahuasca, and doing a lot of yoga—and totally revamped what prosperity meant for me. I designed it and now I'm living it. I keep redesigning it, and I intend on continuing to live in my own perfect, prosperous world."

A

Ashley Black

"When you feel overwhelmed, having a photo of your favorite spot in nature nearby can remind you to take a step back and return to center. You can recalibrate your energy and restore your vitality to complete the goals on your board. When you're manifesting, you want to make sure you're as clear as possible so your authenticity can come through in each and every action you take."

L

Lisa Vrancken

If you'll recall from our chart on masculine and feminine energies, productivity and competition are masculine aspects, whereas relief and cooperation are feminine aspects; humility, then, is the middle point between these aspects. To balance your divine energies means you don't isolate yourself, overwork yourself, put your work or yourself on a pedestal, or forget your place in the grand universe of things.

Some people hold the erroneous idea that humility is something to be avoided—that it's somehow linked to smallness. Far from it. Mother Teresa once said, "If you are humble, nothing will touch you, neither praise nor disgrace, because you know what you are." Humility is not about looking down on yourself or neglecting your needs or wants; it asks that you not only remember your place in the universe, but that you remember that you *have* a place in the universe to begin with. We like to pull from the ancient teachings of the Gita, which considers the sweet spot *nonattachment*. Not detachment—nonattachment. Nonattachment is the center point between overattachment (shorthand for "caring too much") and extreme detachment from everything ("not caring at all"). To put it less elegantly, it's about not buying into your own bullshit. Nonattachment is laying aside the ego, not taking little things too seriously, and enjoying the journey, without any promise of the destination.

What we are asking of you in the closing of our book is that you assess and reassess everything you've worked on so far, keeping in mind the volume of the ego. The ego is the leader of the attachment. So, in order to live life more in the flow, we want to inspire you to keep the ego in check. The ego can derail us from our true self. As you move through your daily life, ask yourself, "Am I doing this for my ego? Or am I doing this for my true self?" It sounds very simple, but as you put this practice in motion, you'll see that our culture has given us some pretty deep samskaras about our ego. As you look at your passions, are they yours, or do they feed the ego? As you examine your purpose(s), are they deep in meaning for your authentic self, or do they excite the ego? As you move into the world of products, are you launching and scaling from a place of groundedness, or is the ego speaking? And most important of all, as you design your prosperity model, is it YOU that is being fulfilled, or the ego?

MOVEMENT #12: EGO CHECK

We've made it to the final Movement. Now lean in.

Closer.

Closer. Let us tell you a secret.

It's not *really* the final Movement.

This book was designed to be read and reread, and we're starting your reread right now. For this Movement, we invite you to return to the very first Movement of the book—and the second, and the third! You probably noticed the blank space at the end of every Movement. Well, in *Choose Your Own Adventure* fashion, we're taking this book out of linear order and time traveling back to all those past Movements.

We hope by this stage in the book you're making waves—even if your waves are small. After coming this far in your journey, it's imperative that you reflect on what has passed, so that you can stay grounded in the present with eyes on the future. Humility doesn't just mean reminding yourself you're not the Queen Bee, it also means not getting hung up on miniscule mistakes you might have made—or even big mistakes. Appreciate the journey with love and respect for the universe and yourself.

Prosperity

For this Movement, we invite you to return to the beginning of the book, reread what you wrote in each Movement, and record your reflection(s) in the blank space provided at the end of the Movement. Return to your brain waves chart, your Golden Circle, your vision board, and so on. How do you think you have grown since then? How have your visions transformed? What, looking back, do you still need to work on and offer yourself grace about? There are no guidelines for what to write in this Movement; let your thoughts and emotions pour forth onto the page. The text box is there to make reflective notes, but feel free to journal as much as you need outside of this book.

As you perform this last Movement in the book, we pray for you, that you will now have a beautifully drawn picture of your life. That you have tangible actions you intend to take. That you have given yourself unbridled permission to live life to the fullest, free of limiting beliefs, free of the ego, free of cultural samskaras. That you will continue to expand and live a rich and zestful life. We hope you approach your life and entrepreneurial path with a newfound sense of passion and purpose that will impact your product journey and explode your prosperity. Now, ladies, go and BE ________________ ________________________ (you get to fill in the blank).

BE...

Gental
Expanding
Caring
Soft
Growing
Loving
Intuitive
Kind
Nurturing
Insightful
Collaborative
Forgiving
Reflective
Sensual
Compassionate
Liberated
Heart Centered
High Vibration
Discerning
Reflective
Wise
Mindful
Mindful
Peaceful
Nurturing
Caring

ABOUT THE AUTHORS

Ashley Black

Ashley Black is an American business mogul who built a nine-figure business from the ground up and still owns 100 percent interest. She was named Entrepreneur of the Year 2020 for Health and Beauty by The American Business

Association. She was named Top Innovator and Inventor of the Year by International Association of Top Professionals in 2019. She is a TEDx speaker, a #1 bestselling author of the breakout hit *The Cellulite Myth: It's not Fat, It's Fascia*, and was named in *Inc.*'s Fastest Growing Companies list.

Black created a revolutionary tool called the FasciaBlaster, a myofascial treating tool. Since its launch in late 2014, Black has successfully launched an entire product suite of holistic care products and has gained over six million fans looking to approach their health and beauty in a new way. Her company, Ashley Black, Inc. has done over $100 million in revenue and has over 1.5 million unique customers. Her products have had over one trillion unique media impressions and have been featured in seven countries and even gained a feature on *Keeping Up with the Kardashians* and *The Today Show*. She has also proven in a peer-reviewed and published scientific study that her tools and methods regenerate fascia tissue, something never achieved before in medicine.

Black began her passion to revolutionize health and beauty as a young girl, unknowingly. Her battle to be healthy and athletic started almost immediately as she was born with juvenile rheumatoid arthritis. She always had a desire for beating the system and her disease by looking for outside-of-the-box solutions. From a very young age, she had the fighting spirit to be healthy, no matter what it took. She overcame JRA, became a competitive gymnast, and even competed in high-level sports in college. All the while she worked in health clubs and nutrition centers and became exposed to the alternative world of natural healing.

She also was a serial achiever, not only beating the odds with her disease, but beating the odds as a teenage business entrepreneur, starting her first business when she was fourteen. She hand-painted clothing and sold it in boutique retail outlets. She used the business to fund her college and love of fast cars.

In her twenties she was stricken with a deadly bone-eating bacteria that once again robbed her of her health. Her right hip, part of her pelvis, and most of the interior of her femur eroded in just a matter of days, and the infection almost killed her. Black had a spiritual awakening during her near-death experience and came back to her existence with a unique knowledge of how the body worked and a zest for educating herself further.

After finding her own solutions and regaining health, her mission became to educate, inspire, and help others. She first began to teach her methods in a sports medicine clinical setting and as an educator providing certifications for bodyworkers and medical professionals. She next became the body guru for pro athletes and celebrities and then set her sights on helping the masses. Since she couldn't physically treat the whole world, she began to conceive of the tools that could, and the Ashley Black product brand was born.

Black has been involved in every facet of her business and now strives to help others maneuver the complex world of launching and scaling businesses. This book with Korie and Lisa was a passion project and a gift for Ashley to share with the world her hard-learned lessons and her heartfelt advice on how to become successful in business and in life. She has moved to Costa Rica and fallen in love with her soulmate, Jordi. She is planning her first exit from her business and looks forward to continuing to pursue health solutions through new ventures and focus on her deep love of the planet and helping preserve it. Her wish for this book is to create a tribe of like-minded, peaceful, successful, mindful women to help raise the greater consciousness.

About the Authors

Korie Minkus

Korie Minkus is an American entrepreneur, advocate for business founders, and a culture-shifter. She is the CEO & founder of Rock Your Product®, the number one global product business advisory and growth training company. As a leading global brand strategist and physical product-based business-scale expert, Korie spent twenty-five years as a consumer product Fortune 500 thought-action executive, prior to starting Rock Your Product® in 2017. She has launched and scaled hundreds of products and worked with brands generating billions of dollars in e-commerce and brick-and-mortar revenue. Korie has partnered, sold, invested in, or negotiated with emerging and legacy brands like Unilever, Walt Disney Co., 3M, Johnson & Johnson, Honest Company, Procter & Gamble, and L'Oréal Paris.

With a passionate, heart-centered approach, Korie inspires, consults, advises, and mentors entrepreneurs. She has trained over one hundred thousand businesses, delivering results through award-winning systems and generating profitable market-share growth for entrepreneurs globally. Korie leads business owners to strategic clarity and confident decision-making by providing proven tools for measurable scale and the sequence of necessary steps for success. As an international speaker, Korie is a sought-after expert in physical products, consumer psychology, and fast multipliers through channel distribution. Korie's strategic partnerships have spanned the top ten worldwide retailers, including Amazon, Walmart, Costco, Kroger, and Walgreens Boots Alliance, among thousands of others.

Korie has collaborated and been mentored by some of the biggest business leaders on the planet, including Marcus Lemonis, the CEO of Camping World and star of CNBC's *The Profit*; the founder of Facebook Live Randi Zuckerberg;

Kevin Harrington, the original Shark from *Shark Tank*; legendary motivational speaker Les Brown; Lisa Nichols, star of the film *The Secret*; and Dean Graziosi and Tony Robbins of Knowledge Broker Blueprint. The list includes some of the greatest business leaders in retail, including Doug McMillon, president and CEO of Walmart Inc.; Mark L. Butler, founder of Ollie's Bargain Outlet at a $3.1 billion net worth; and Pennie Clark Ianniciello, thirty-year veteran Media Buyer for Costco Wholesale Corporation, a top-three leading retailer worldwide. These partnerships and friends have shared their secrets of success, as they seek a similar mission of multipliers.

With impact and conscious leadership at the forefront of her mission, Korie encourages problem solving, worth expansion, and getting uncomfortable to be unstoppable. She has conducted over five thousand presentations, attended hundreds of global trade shows, and managed international business in thirty-two countries. Korie is retained, as a trusted advisor, to service emerging and legacy brands from customization in the areas of market relevancy, branding, retention systems, sales strategies, distribution channel optimization, to capitalization, exit strategies, and M&A activities. Korie, in true form, finds every opportunity to personalize the approach and innovate how business is conducted.

Korie was a competitive figure skater for twenty-two years and learned the love of healthy living, the spirit of competition, dedication, and discipline from a very young age. She is the wife of her high school sweetheart and the mom of two boys both focused on their own athletic and academic achievements. She is recognized by her friends as the "Garland Girl," with her dedicated commitment to linking like-minded souls together. As the loving big sister of Kane, founder of Industry Rockstar®, and of her adored older brother Kirk, a vascular surgeon and interventional radiologist, her family system was rooted in deep love, a commitment to continued growth, and a fierce belief in living life to the fullest.

Korie is skilled and certified in Landmark Education and neuro-linguistic programming (NLP), a method dedicated to improved individual productivity, communication, rapport building techniques, personal development, and transformational work. Korie is a sought-after board member with several global companies across the media, digital, technology, medical, and product industries.

Korie's operating belief system: "The more you share with the universe, the more the universe will share with you."

Lisa Vrancken

Lisa Vrancken is an award-winning TV producer, media expert, and documentary filmmaker with over two decades of expertise as an internationally renowned brand strategist. She crafts commercials and product videos to create brand awareness and drive revenue, providing clients with strategic, full-service video production from start to finish.

In her current role as executive vice president of Fortune Media Group, Inc., she spearheads programming for Shark Discoveries and AsSeenOnTv.pro with prominent host Kevin Harrington—the original Shark from the Emmy award–winning entrepreneurial-themed reality TV show, *Shark Tank.*

As the executive VP of a media company breaking barriers and redefining the art of corporate videos, she produces standout visual media for budding startups and the world's largest companies, overseeing everything from concept to production to distribution on cable television networks and digital platforms around the world.

She's also the architect of the Innovator's Think Tank, a quarterly global event for product innovators and entrepreneurs. She's been a catalyst for the successful trajectories of hundreds of diverse brands in distinct product categories.

Specializing in TV, digital marketing, and branded entertainment, Lisa masterfully weaves interdepartmental connections for production, drives cross-platform revenue strategies, creates relevant content, and develops engaging video and commercial advertising for clients of all stripes. She's a co-founder of Raw Form LLC with co-author Korie Minkus and beauty expert Sarah Eggenberger, specializing in bridging raw ingredient suppliers with independent brands and private retail labels. In 2021, she founded BE...Creative Agency LLC, which provides expert consulting in branding and marketing strategies, events, and visual media.

A globally sought-after product consultant, marketing expert, and public speaker, Lisa has mentored hundreds on their entrepreneurial journeys. With a background in law and human rights advocacy, her mission is to mentor women from all walks of life to stand in their power, while providing them with the tools and frameworks to communicate their truths through the art of visual storytelling. Lisa's philosophy of life: "On your own journey of discovery, touch as many souls, uplift as many lives, and make a positive impact on as many people as possible."